Çocuklar İçin Kısa Hikayelerle Değerler D

Çalışmak

Bilinç ve Karakter Gelişimi

Erdinç Yarışı Kazanır

Erdinç, her zaman iyi bir koşucu olmak istiyordu fakat bacakları akranlarına göre biraz güçsüzdü. Buna çok üzülüyordu.

Bir gün bahçede üzgün bir şekilde otururken annesi geldi ve "Benim tatlı oğlum, neden ağlıyor?" diye sordu. Erdinç annesine, "İyi bir koşucu olmak, yarışlara katılabilmek istiyorum. Fakat ne zaman koşmayı denesem istediğim kadar hızlı olamıyorum" diye açıkladı üzüntüsünü.

Bunun üzerine annesi Erdinç'e doktora gitmek isteyip istemediğini sordu. Böylece neden istediğini kadar hızlı koşamadığını anlayabileceklerini ve doktorun ona yardımcı olabileceğini söyledi. Erdinç hastaneye gitmeye karar verdi.

Doktor, Erdinç'i muayene etti ve eğer çalışırsa Erdinç'in da iyi bir koşucu olabileceğini söyledi. Bunu duyan Erdinç çok sevindi. Çok çalışarak bir koşucu olmaya karar verdi.

Her sabah antrenman yapan Erdinç, gün geçtikçe bacaklarının güçlendiğini ve daha hızlı koşabildiğini fark ediyordu. Bir koşu yarışmasına katıldı ve birinci oldu. Çalışıp başardığı için çok mutluydu.

Ne öğrendik?

Başarıya giden yol, çalışmaktan geçer.

Küçük Karıncalar ve Tahıl

Doli çalışkan, küçük bir karıncaydı. Ailesiyle birlikte küçük kalelerinde mutlu bir hayat sürüyordu.

Kış yaklaşıyordu. Diğer tüm karıncalar gibi kışlık beslenmelerini sağlayabilmeleri için Doli'nin de evlerine tahıl taşımasının vakti gelmişti.

Tahıllarsa Doli ve onun gibi küçük karıncalar için ağırdı. Doli ise tahılları taşımaya kararlıydı çünkü ailesine yardım edebilmek istiyordu. Bir plan yapmalıydı. Aklına bir fikir geldi.

Eğer tahılları daha küçük parçalara ayırıp taşırlarsa yavru karıncalar da tahılları kolayca taşıyabilirdi. Böylece ailelerine yardımcı olabileceklerdi. Hemen bu fikrini arkadaşlarıyla paylaştı.

Arkadaşları bu fikri çok sevdiler. Hep birlikte çalışmaya koyuldular. Onların da tahıl evlerine tahıl taşıması ailelerini çok mutlu etmişti. Yavru karıncalarına teşekkür ettiler.

Ne Öğrendik?

Hep birlikte çalışmak daha çok başarı getirir.

Oyun

Ferdi çalışkan bir öğrenciydi. Bir gün, doğum günü için ailesi ona bir oyun hediye etmişlerdi. Ferdi bu armağanları için çok mutlu oldu ve onlara teşekkür etti.

Oyun oynamayı çok sevmişti. Neredeyse her fırsatta oyun oynamaya başlamıştı. O kadar çok zaman ayırıyordu ki ödevlerini yapması gerektiğinde bile kendisini oyundan alamıyordu.

Bir gün ödevlerini yapmak için odasına gitti ve defterini açtı.

O kadar çok ödevi vardı ki hepsini yapabileceği zamanı kalmamıştı.

Ertesi gün ödevlerinin hepsini bitirememiş olduğunu gören öğretmeni, Ferdi'ye "Ödevlerine gerektiği kadar zaman ayıramamış olman beni çok üzdü" dedi. Ferdi hatasını anlamıştı.

Oyun oynayarak eğlenmek istiyordu fakat başarısız bir öğrenci olmak istemiyordu. O günden sonra oyun oynamaya olduğu gibi ödevlerini yapmaya da zaman ayırmaya dikkat etti. Hem eğleniyor hem de başarılı oluyordu.

Ne Öğrendik?

Oyun oynarken, ders çalışmayı ihmal etmemeliyiz.

Gayretli Maymun

Monti, arkadaşlarıyla birlikte bir adada yaşıyordu. Mevsim değişiyordu ve yakında adaya yağmurlar yağmaya başlayacaktı.

Adadaki tüm maymunlar, yağmurlardan korunabilmek için kendilerine kurumuş otlardan ev yapmaya başladılar. Monti'ninse başka bir fikri vardı. Evini taşlardan yapacaktı. Böylece şiddetli yağmurlardan daha iyi korunabilirdi.

Fakat taşları bulmak, otları bulmaktan zordu. Daha ağır oldukları için taşıması da daha zordu. Onun evini taşlarla yaptığını gören maymunlardan biri, "Bu kadar kendini yormana gerek var mı Monti? Sen de bizim gibi çabuk biten evlerden bir tane yapsana" dedi.

Sonunda yağmurlar başlamıştı. Öyle şiddetli yağıyordu ki maymunların evleri sular altında kalmıştı. Monti'nin uzun zaman çalışarak yaptığı taş evi ise sapasağlamdı.

Neyse ki Monti tüm arkadaşlarını misafir edebilecek kadar büyük bir ev yapmıştı. Tüm arkadaşlarını evine çağırdı. Yağmurlar bitip güneş tekrar açana kadar hep birlikte kaldılar. Arkadaşları Monti'ye çok teşekkür ettiler.

Ne Öğrendik?

Sadece bugün için değil, geleceği düşünerek çalışmalıyız.

Çalışkan Oduncu

Bir gün yaşlı bir oduncu omzuna yüklediği ağır kütüklerle evine doğru gidiyordu.

Yolda giderken cömert bir genç adam ile karşılaştı. Genç adam, "Hepsini taşımak zor olmalı. Size yardım etmeme izin verin." dedi.

Oduncu genç adama teşekkür etti ve "Unutma genç adam, eğer başarılı bir hayat sürmek istiyorsan her işini kendin yapmaya çalışmalısın. Başkalarına yük olmamalısın. Yaşlı olmamdan dolayı böyle bir teklif yaptığını biliyorum. Fakat, yine de bunu hatırlatmak istedim. Biz böyle yetiştirildik. Hep çok çalıştık." dedi. Yaşlı adam kendisine yardım etmek isteyen gence, yükünün birazını verdi ve yola devam ettiler.

Ne Öğrendik?

Başarılı olmak için her işimizi kendimiz yapmalıyız. Kendi işlerini yapamayan hasta ve yaşlı kişilere yardım etmeliyiz.

SUPERBOOK of Things TO MAKE

Pia Hsiao
Neil Lorimer

Macdonald & Jane's

CONTENTS

1 tape measure
2 hammer
3 pliers
4 cutting tool
5 clippers
6 paint brush
7 paint brush
8 pincers
9 saw
10 screwdriver
11 drill
12 fretsaw
13 scissors
14 crochet hook
15 file
16 punch
17 knitting needles
18 nails
19 drawing pins

1
2
3
4
5
6
7
8
9
10
11
12
13
14
15
16
17
18
19

USEFUL HINTS

How to cut

Use a ruler and sharp knife.
Cut on a cutting board which will not be damaged.

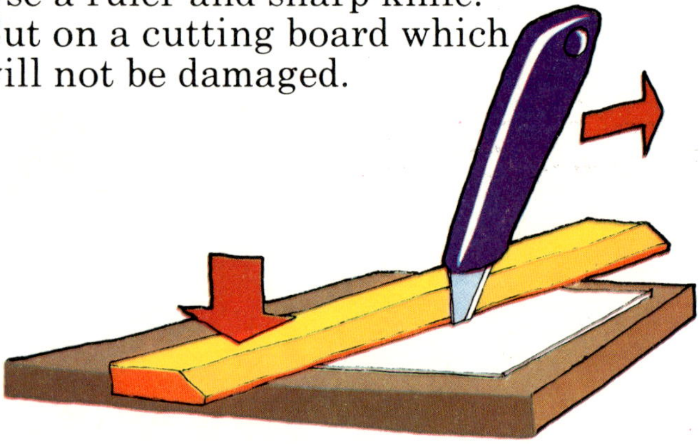

How to fold

Score not more than halfway through the card along the line which you want to fold. Use a ruler. The card will fold easily along the scored line.

How to enlarge designs

When you want to enlarge a picture, draw a squared grid over the original picture first. Then draw a squared grid on a piece of paper of the size you require.
Copy the picture square by square on to the larger grid.

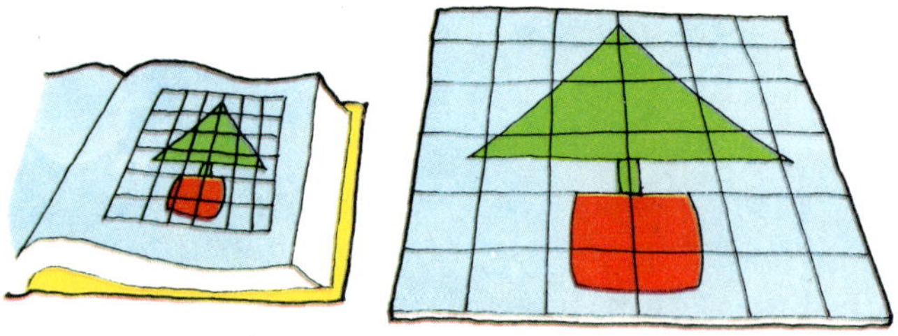

How to snip

Always mark out the fold and cutting line first.

How to make holes

To make holes in wood, use a drill.
To make holes in card, use a sharp knife or punch.
To make holes in thin metal, use a nail and hammer.

How to glue

Always put glue on both the surfaces which you want to stick together. Spread the glue all over the surfaces with a piece of card.

How to use colour

White or light colours make things seem larger. Dark colours make things seem smaller. Soft colours, like fawn, beige and maroon, are quiet and relaxing. Vivid, pure colours appear more alive and active. Some colours, like reds and oranges, appear warmer than blues and greens.

Painting

1 Make sure that the surface you are painting is clean. Wood can be cleaned with sandpaper. Metal or plastic can be cleaned with turpentine or white spirits. If you only need to remove grease and grubbiness, use detergent and water. Make sure that your brush is thoroughly clean too. Clean it immediately after use, especially if you have been painting with enamels.

2 When you use light colours, paint the surface with a white undercoat first.

3 Choose the right type of paint for your material. Gouache and acrylics (which come in vivid colours) are good for cardboard, paper, wood, stone or acetate. Acrylics are washable; gouache is not. Both dry quickly and can be varnished. Lacquer or enamel paint can be used on cardboard, wood, metal, plastic and glass. They can be diluted with white spirits or turpentine and put on in thin coats of colour. They take from 3 to 10 hours to dry.
Inks give vivid, transparent colours. Use them on any slightly absorbent surface like cardboard or wood.

4 Before you start painting, always put down newspapers to catch drips and spills. If you are using a paint spray, you will need even more newspaper.

5 Make sure you put the lids back firmly on all the paint tins when you finish.

Warning: Keep turpentine, white spirits and other solvents away from heat or any open flame.

Warning: When working with lacquer or varnish, always make sure that the windows are open and the room is well ventilated.

STORING THINGS

PENCIL HOLDER

You will need:

a large tin lid or circle of heavy card
paper or plastic cups
paints and paint brush
cutting tool
glue

1 Paint the tin lid or circle of heavy card all over in one colour of your own choice.

2 Paint the cups in one colour or in different colours and let them dry before going on to stage 3.

3 Cut the holes for the pencils by cutting crosses on the base of each cup as shown in the diagram.

4 Glue the cups to the tray.
Push your pencils through the holes in the cups.
This holder could equally well be used for pens, biros or felt tip pens.

GREAT BRITAIN

STORAGE POCKETS

You will need:

1·5 metre of canvas for backing
1 metre of canvas for pockets
paper pencil scissors
needle, pins and buttonhole thread
rod about 80 cm long

1 Enlarge each piece onto the paper for your pattern. To draw curved shapes, put a plate onto the paper and trace round it.

2 Pin the pattern onto the canvas.

3 Cut out the canvas pieces.

4 Cut 3 pieces of canvas for the supporting loops.

5 Sew the loops onto the backing.

6 Sew small pockets onto large ones.

7 Sew the large pockets onto the canvas backing.

8 Slip the rod through the loops.

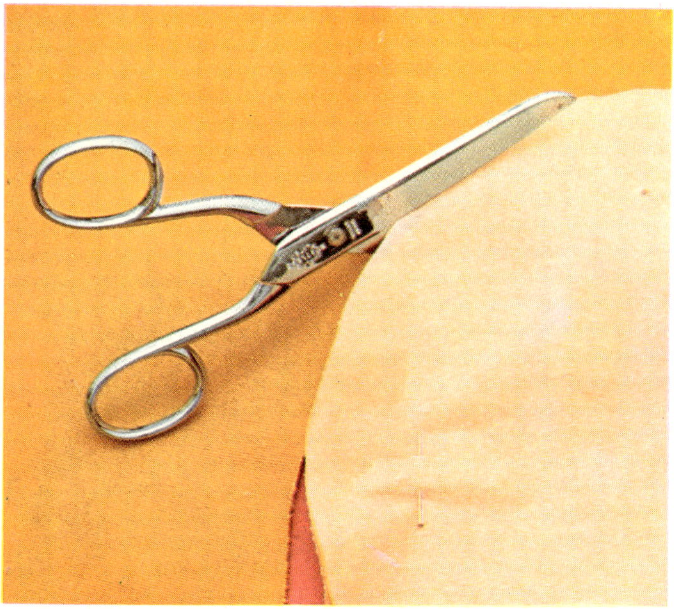

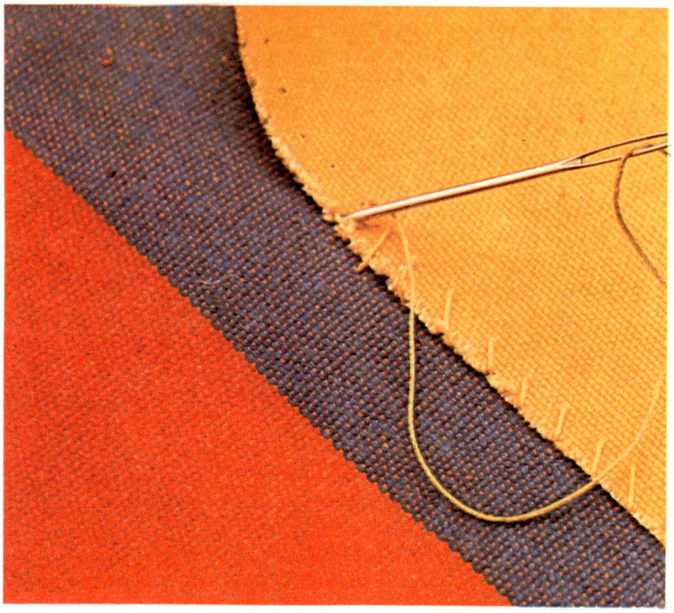

STORAGE SYSTEM

You will need:

a number of large sweet, paint or food tins
paints
paint brush
strong coloured sticky tape

1 Clean the cans thoroughly inside and out.

2 Paint the outside of each can a different bright colour.

3 Paint the inside of all the cans the same colour.

4 Bind the cans together with the sticky tape.
Depending on how many cans you have, you can make a pyramid with 6, 10 or 15 cans. You can also make a circular system using 7 or 13 cans.

1

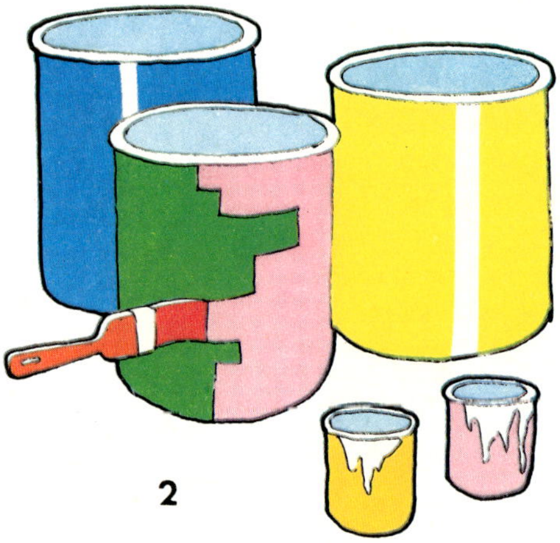

2

3

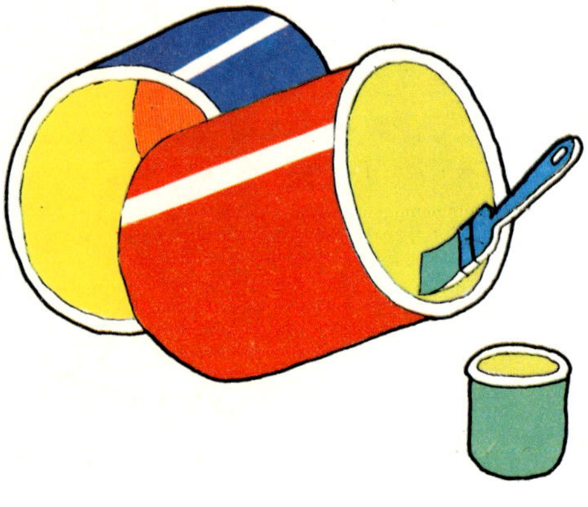

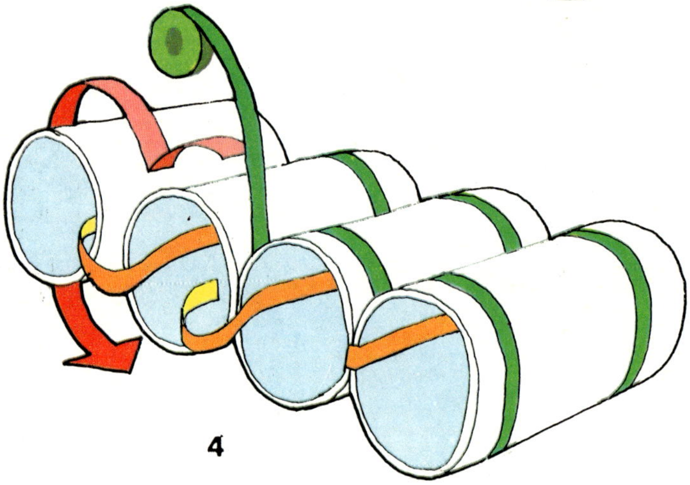

4

a

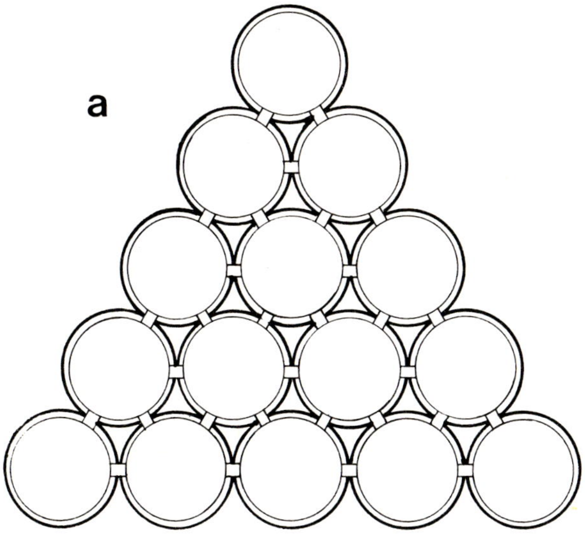

b

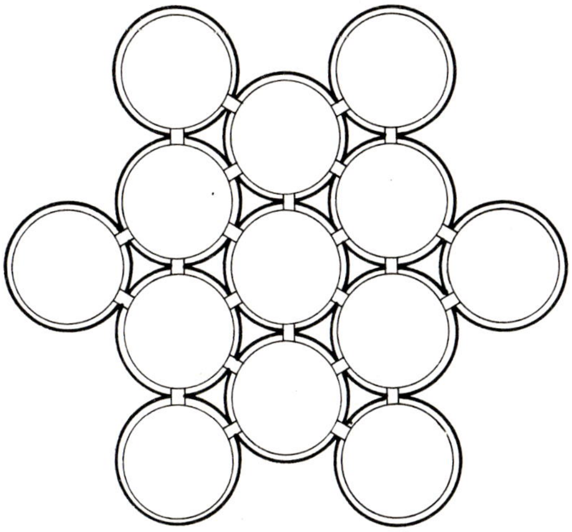

PAINTED CHEST

You will need:

chest or wooden box
white undercoat paint
paints
paint brush
pencil

1 Clean the chest thoroughly.

2 Paint the chest all over in undercoat to hide any marks and give a good surface to work on.

3 Draw your chosen design onto the dry white undercoat.

4 Paint in the design. Start with the background.

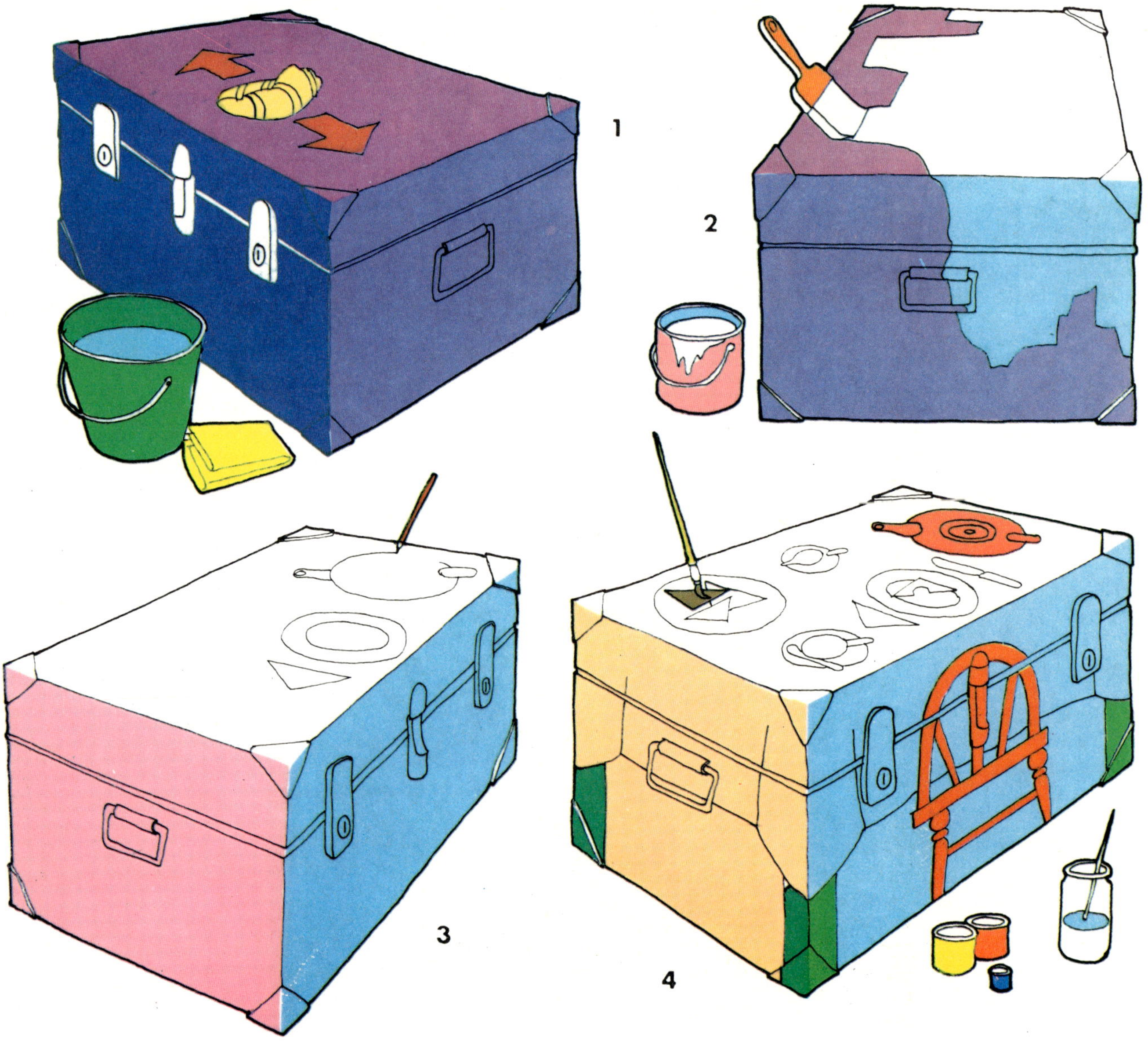

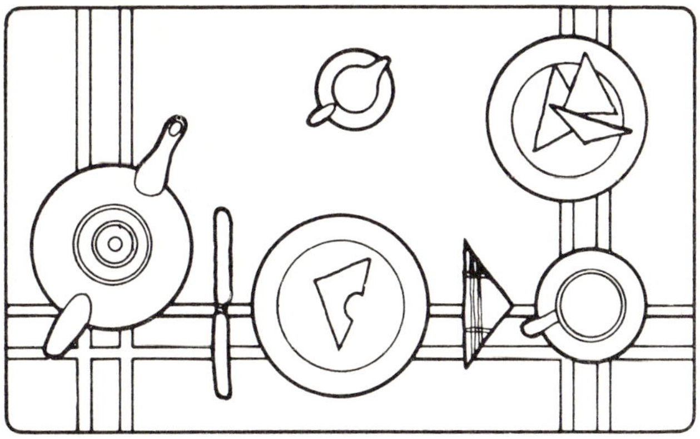

The diagram shows designs for the top and front of the chest.

LADLE HOOKS

You will need:

soup ladles
enamel paints and brush
thick wool   glue
wooden block
strong coloured sticky tape

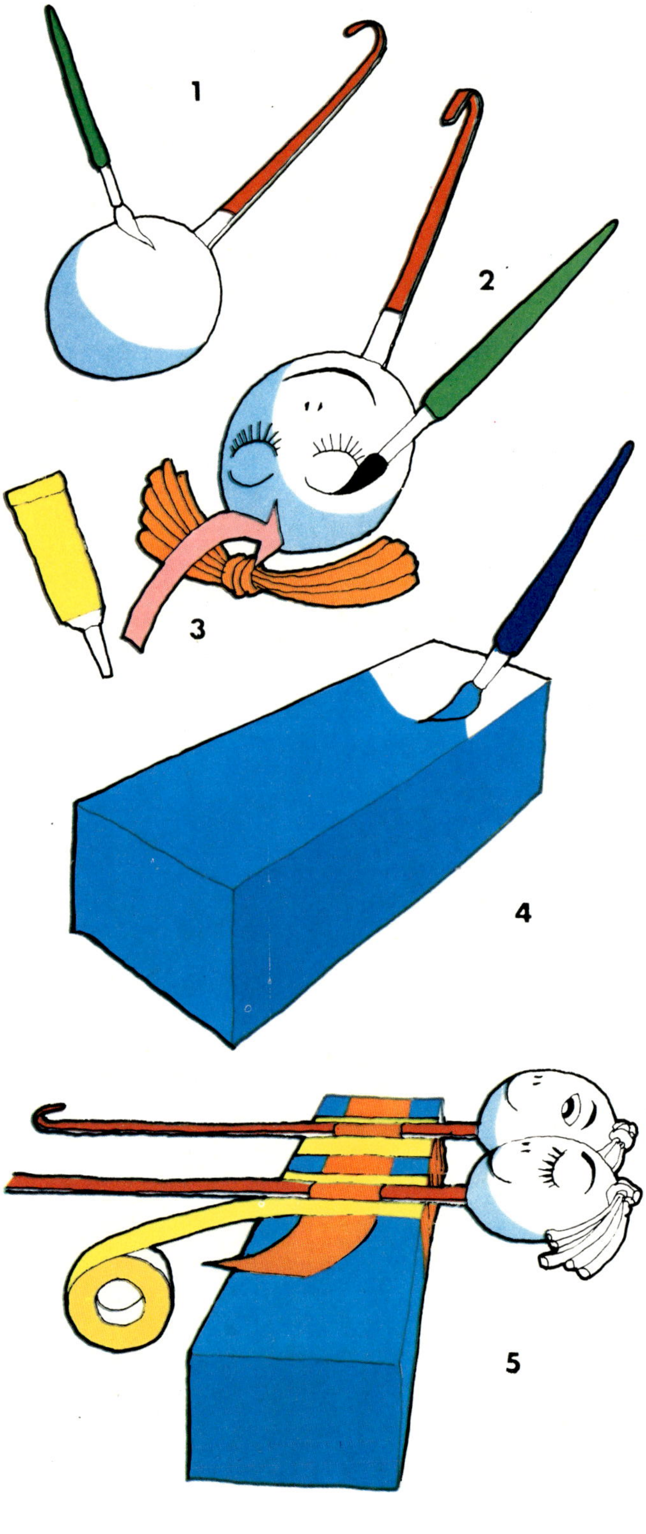

1 Paint the ladles all over in a plain colour. Let the paint dry thoroughly before going on to the next stage.

2 Paint faces with different expressions onto the back of each of the spoons.

3 Tie short lengths of wool into a knot and glue to the ladle for hair. The wool can be any colour in order to change the appearance of each face.

4 Paint the wooden block.

5 Using the coloured tape, stick the ladles onto the wooden block. Fix the hanging rail to the wall.

VENEERED BOXES

You will need:

cardboard box
wood veneer
pencil   glue
cutting tool
lacquer and brush

1 and 2 Use a ready made cardboard box or make one as shown here. Transfer your chosen design onto the surface you want to cover.

3 and 4 Trace the parts of the design onto different coloured or textured veneers. Cut out the pieces.

5 Glue the pieces of veneer onto the design on the surface of the box.

6 and 7 Sand the surface of the box. Apply a thin coat of lacquer.

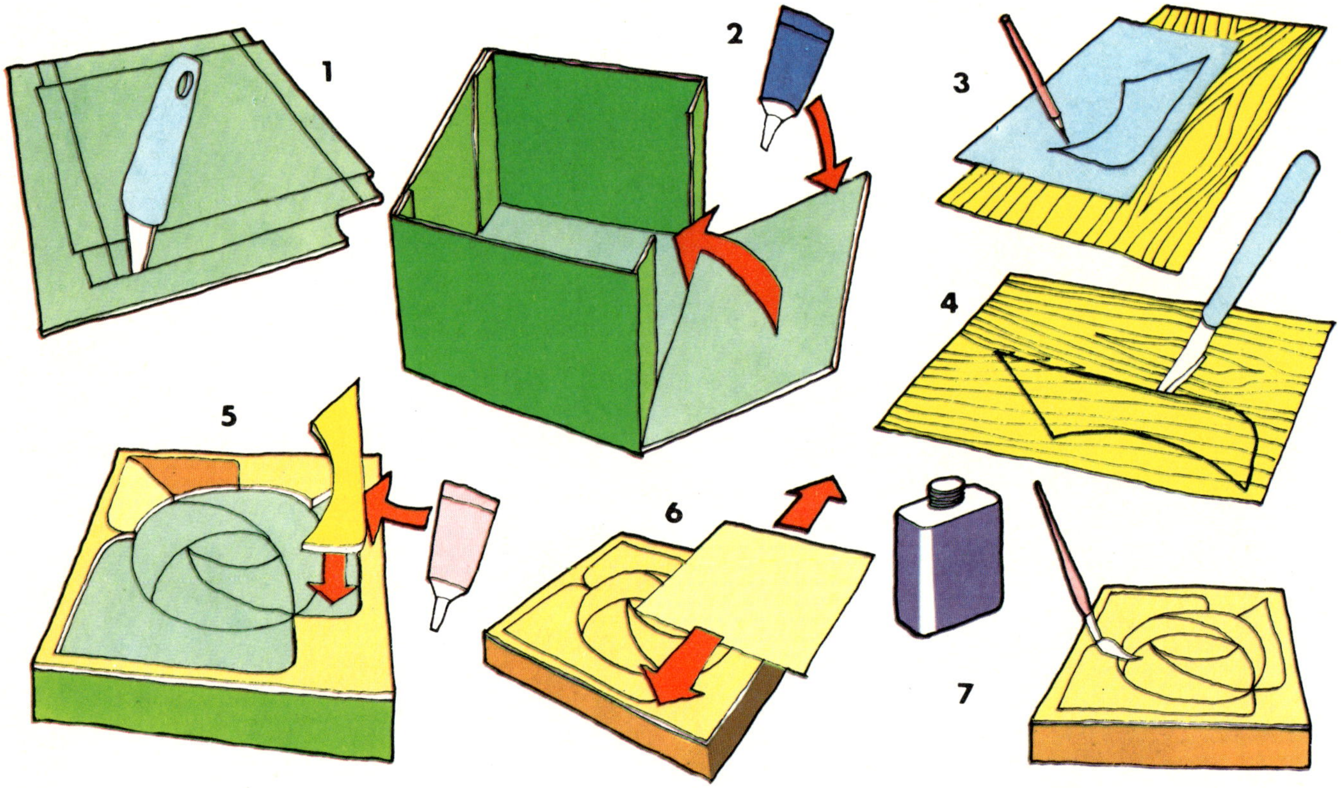

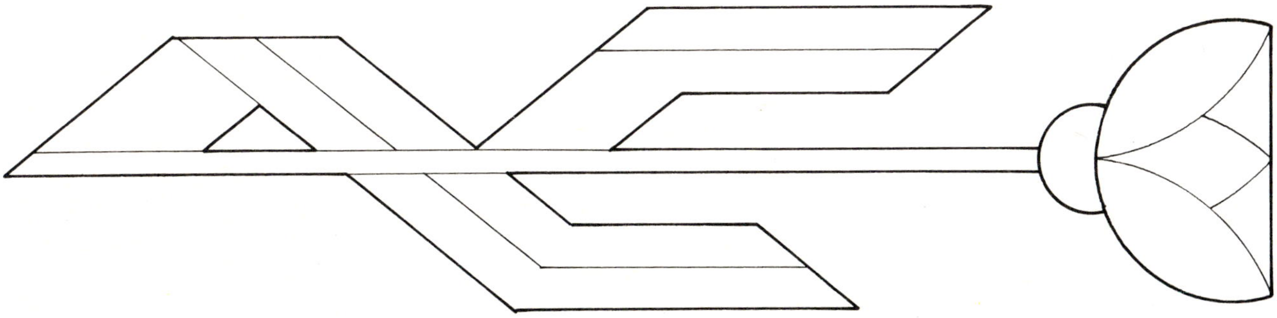

DESK ENGINE

You will need:

light plywood · tube · wood blocks
fretsaw · vice · hammer
paints and brush · glue
cutting tool · coloured tape

1

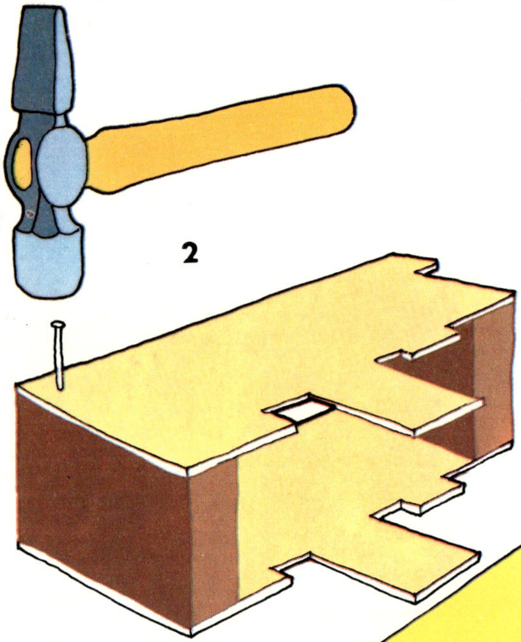

2

3

4

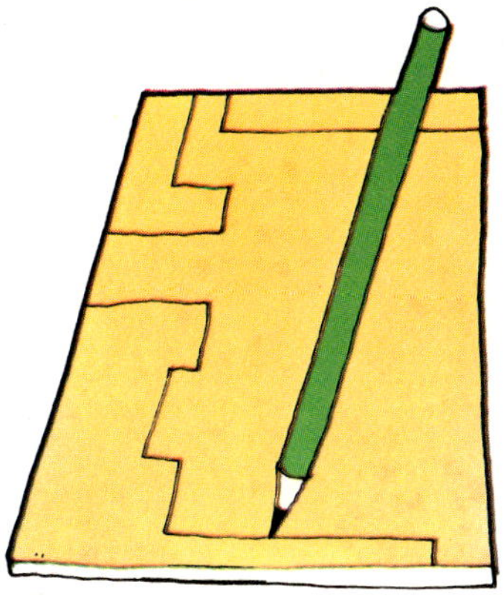

1 Draw the outline of the engine on to the plywood. Hold the card firmly in the vice while you cut around the outline with the fretsaw.

2 Glue the sides and the wood blocks together to make the body

3 Cut the tube into two bits wider than the engine. Cut slots in the tubes the width of the engine apart. Fix the engine into the slots.

4 Paint the engine and decorate it with strips of coloured tape.

TELEPHONE LIST

You will need:

heavy card
paper
pencil
cutting tool
glue
paint and paintbrush

1 Enlarge the shape shown here so that the total width is about 13 cm. Cut it out carefully

2 Score along the dotted lines. Fold the card as shown to form a box. Glue the overlapping edges of the box together firmly.

3 Cut 26 sheets of card wide enough to fit snugly into the box. The height of the first card (for the letter A) should be a little higher than the front of the box and the other cards should each be 1 cm taller on the left through to Z.

Cut out the tops of the cards: O–Z in the shapes of clouds; L–N in the shapes of hills and mountains; A–K into gentle slopes and houses. Paint the scenes on to the cards and the front of the box. You can give the impression of more depth by colouring the foreground stronger and the background weaker. Label the top left hand corners of the cards from A to Z. The cards are now ready for you to enter the names, telephone numbers and addresses of your friends on to them.

NEEDLEWORK TRAIN

You will need:

2 shoe boxes
wooden spoon
cutting tool
glue   pencils
paint and paint brush
cloth   string
corks

This colourful train is designed to contain all your needlework so that you can find whatever you need easily.

1 Take the lid from one of the boxes and cut it so that it fits as shown in the diagram.
Glue it in place.

2 Draw the design for the train on each box.
Paint in the design.

3 Cut a small hole at either end of both boxes. Tie a knot in one end of the piece of string. Thread the string through one box and into the hole at one end of the other to link the train together. Tie another knot inside the box to hold the string in position.
Cut slits in the lid of one box to hold the pencils for the reels of thread.

4 Make the wooden spoon into a pin cushion by sewing a pad of cloth over the bowl of the spoon.
Push the wooden spoon through the hole at the front of the train.

5 Paint some corks and glue them to the bottom of the boxes for wheels. You could use circles of heavy card instead of corks for the wheels.

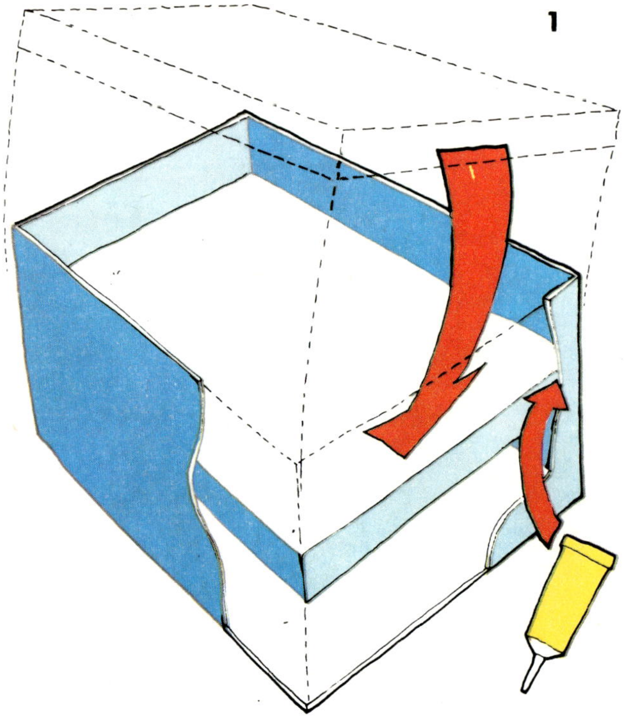

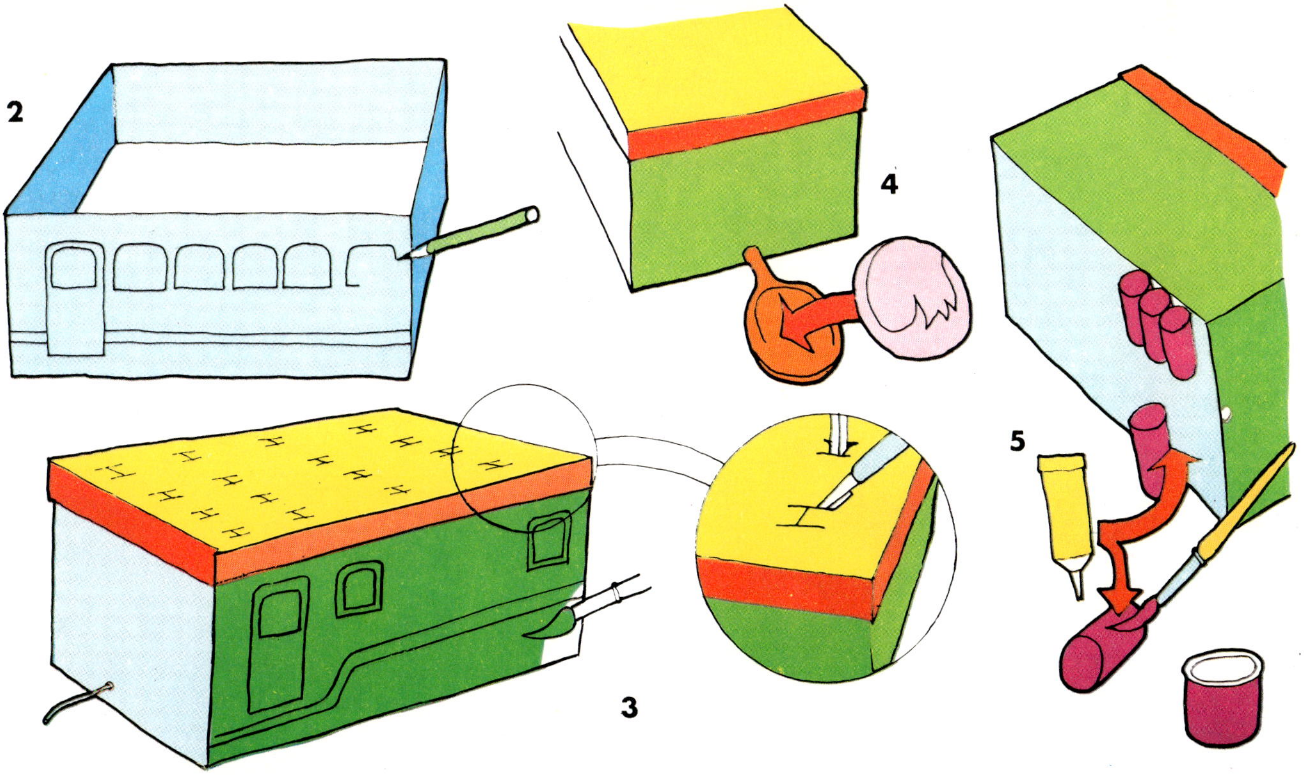
2
4
5
3

LAMPS

TRIANGLE LAMP

You will need:

lengths of balsa wood 2 cm × 2 cm
coping saw   glue
thin and thick card   tracing paper
4 bottle tops
light fitting

On the subject of electrical fittings you must take advice from someone who can show you the safest possible method of fixing the fitting.

1 Cut 6 lengths of wood 45 cm long. Cut the ends off each at a 60° angle. Make sure that each piece is exactly the same length.

2 Glue 3 pieces of wood together to form a triangle. Glue the 3 other pieces to form a second triangle.

3 Cut 3 pieces of wood 15 cm long. Glue these to join the two triangles.

4 Using the triangular face of the frame as a pattern, draw a triangle on the card. This is the lamp front.

5 Cut out this triangle. Using a round lid as a pattern, draw and cut out 3 circles in the triangle.

6 Glue the piece of tracing paper over the back of these round holes to diffuse the light.

7 Using the two rectangular sides of the frame as patterns, draw and cut out two pieces of card. Cut a piece of thicker card for the bottom. Glue all the pieces of card onto the lamp frame. Fix lamp fitting.

8 Glue the four bottle tops onto base.

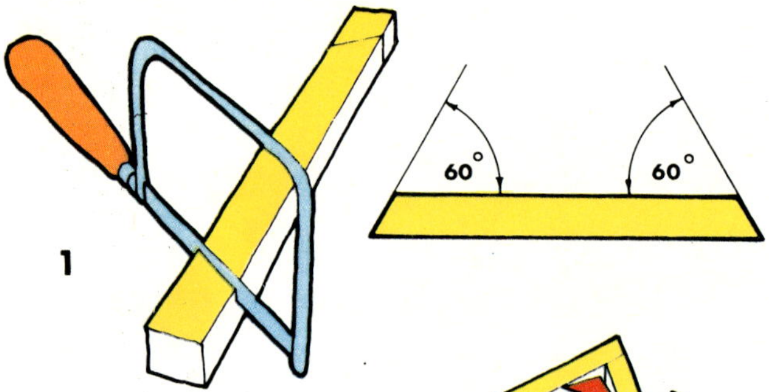

1

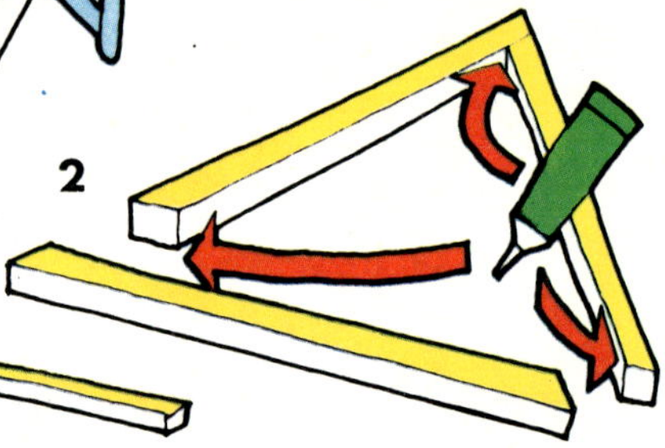
2

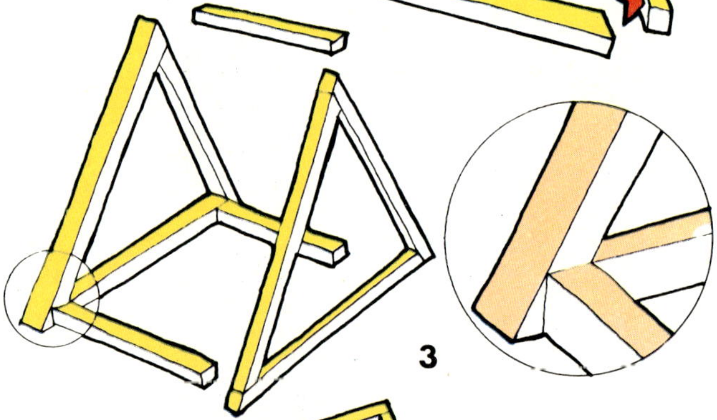
3

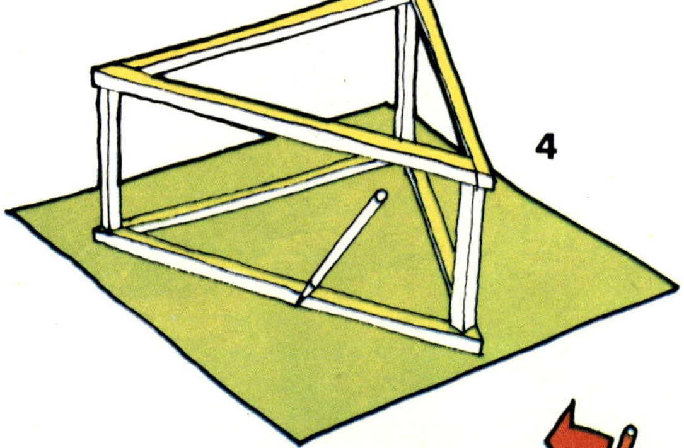
4

5

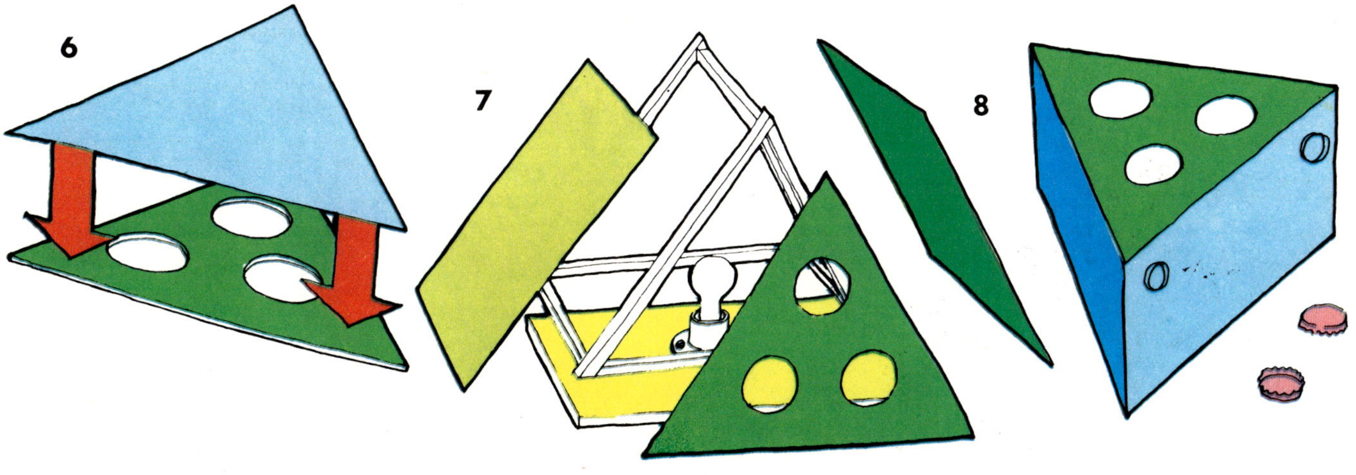
6
7
8

PAINT CAN LAMP

You will need:

a large paint can
white and coloured paints
paint brush   pencil
heavy card
strong nail
hammer
light fitting

1 Clean the paint can thoroughly. Paint the inside of the can with the white paint which will reflect the light.

2 Mark out your design in pencil on the sides and bottom of the paint can.

3 Punch holes along the sides of the can with the nail or a punch. Put a block of wood inside the can while you are hammering or you will dent the surface of the lamp.

4 Paint the outside of the lamp with the coloured paint.

5 Cut out a circle the same diameter as the paint can from the heavy card. Cut a notch in one side big enough to take the flex of the light fitting. Paint the card.
Fix the light fitting onto the card so that the flex fits into the notch.
Place the can over the light fitting.

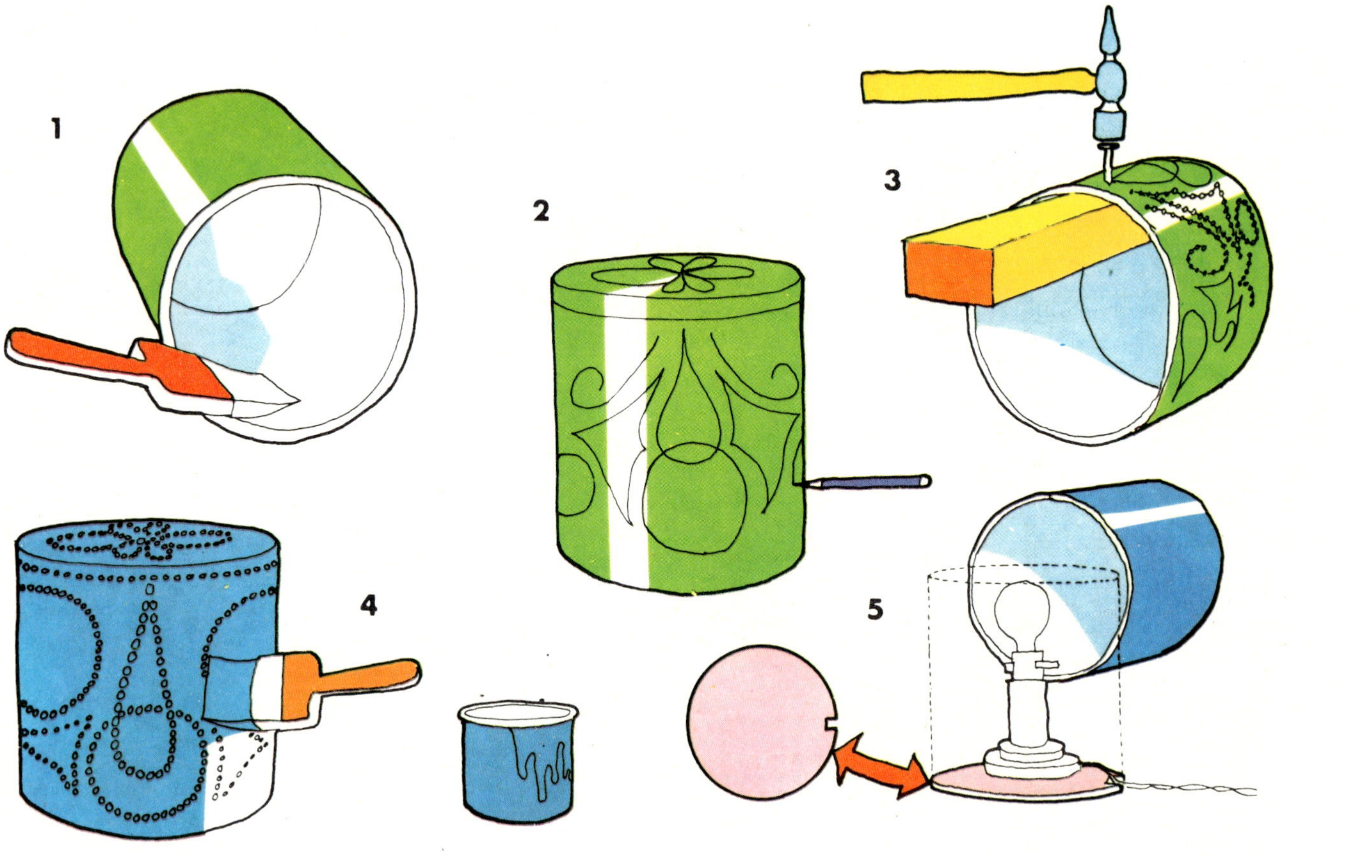

PING PONG LIGHT

You will need:

lots of ping pong balls
paint and paint brush
needle thread
card sticky tape
cutting tool

1 Paint the ping pong balls in a multitude of different colours. Allow them to dry thoroughly.

2 Making a small knot in the end of the varying lengths of thread, push the needle through the balls. Pull the knot through the lower hole so that it is hidden inside the ball.

3 Cut a large disc of card. Make a hole in the middle for the light cord to pass through. Thread the ends of the threads through the disc and sellotape them down as shown, so that the ping pong balls hang round the light at different levels. Fit the card disc to the ceiling.

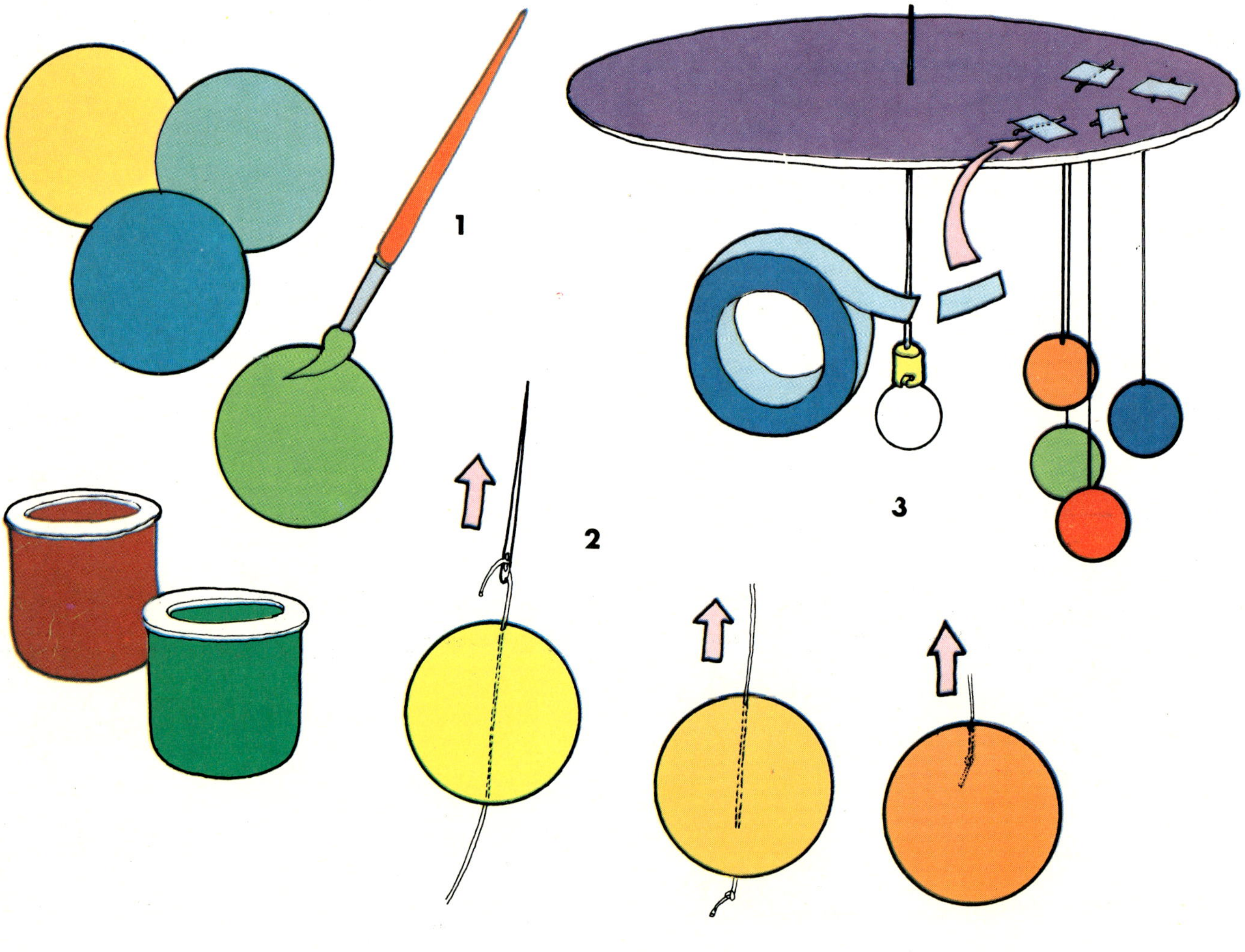

COLOURED PAPER LAMP

You will need:

6 different coloured pieces of cartridge paper
thin plywood
saw
cutting tool
light fitting

The diagram on the right gives the dimensions for the various parts of this lamp.
As with the other lamps in this section, you will need help with fixing the light fitting to make sure that it is completely safe.

1 Cut out the base of the lamp from the plywood shown in orange in the diagram.

2 Measure and cut out the pieces of coloured cartridge paper. Cut one piece the dimensions of the pale orange piece. Cut 2 pieces each with the dimensions of the 5 other pieces shown in the diagram.

3 Score fold lines about 1·5 cm from the end of each piece of paper. Fold the ends down along these fold lines.

4 Fix the light fitting into the plywood base.
Glue each sheet of paper to the plywood base.
Allow the glue to dry thoroughly before you turn on the light so that the pieces of paper will be firmly fixed and will not shift.

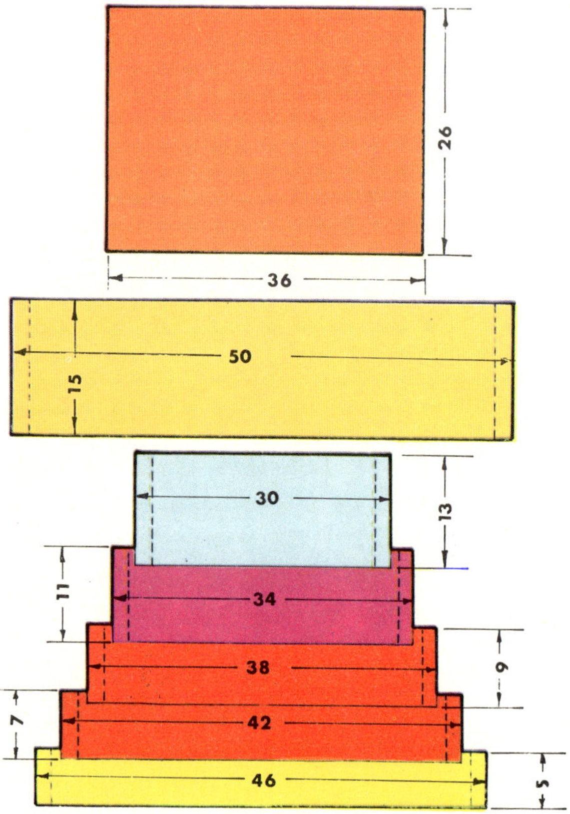

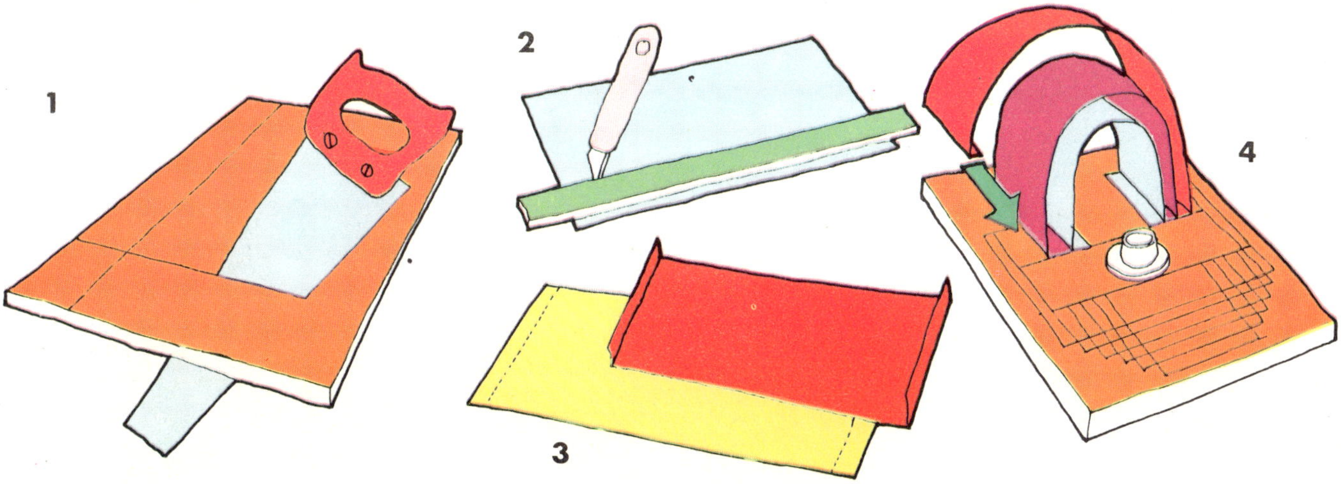
1
2
3
4

FRUIT LAMP

You will need:

cardboard box   cardboard
ruler   pencil   glue   cutting tool
paint and paint brush
sheets of cellophane
tracing paper   light fitting

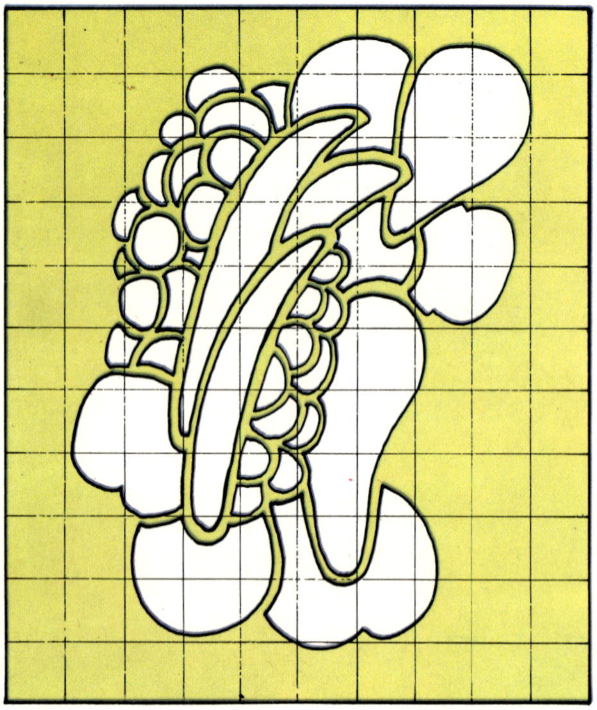

This lamp will be even more effective if you use a material like acetate or cinemoid as they will not buckle in the warmth of the light as cellophane may do. You may like to experiment first with cellophane which is cheaper. You can always take it off later and fix the stronger materials in its place.

1 Cut a piece of card large enough to fit onto the front of the box.
The top drawing shows the grid diagram for enlarging the picture. Repeat this grid onto the card and enlarge the design onto it.

2 Cut out the centre of each piece of fruit very carefully. Take care to keep the edges as smooth as possible and not to cut through the card between each piece.
Paint the piece of card.

3 Glue pieces of different coloured cellophane to the back of each piece of fruit.
Then glue a sheet of tracing paper behind the cut out picture. This will diffuse the light.

4 Cut out the bottom of the box. Paint the box to match the fruit panel.

5 Glue the fruit panel onto the front of the box. Fix the light fitting in behind the panel.

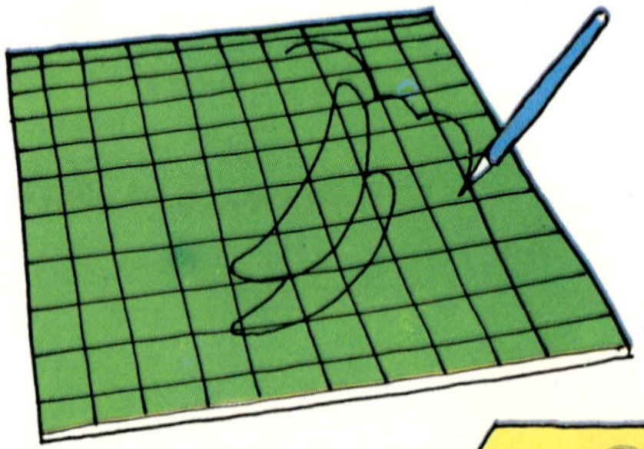
1

2

3

4
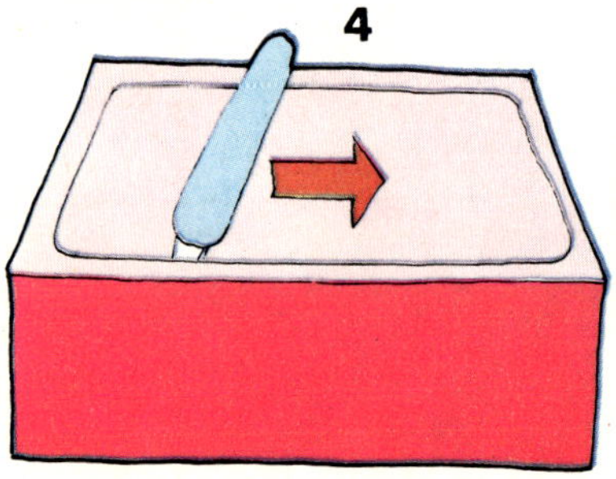

5

TOYS AND GAMES

HORSE RACING

You will need:

a sheet of plywood
length of 20 mm × 45 mm wood
heavy card dowel rod
saw cutting tool staples
drill glue string paint

1 Paint the plywood track green.

2 Saw the wood into 9 cm blocks (2 for the finishing post, the rest for horses). Paint in different colours.

3 Cut horses out of the card. Colour to match the blocks.
Cut slots in the blocks. Glue the horses into the slots. Fix a staple to each block.

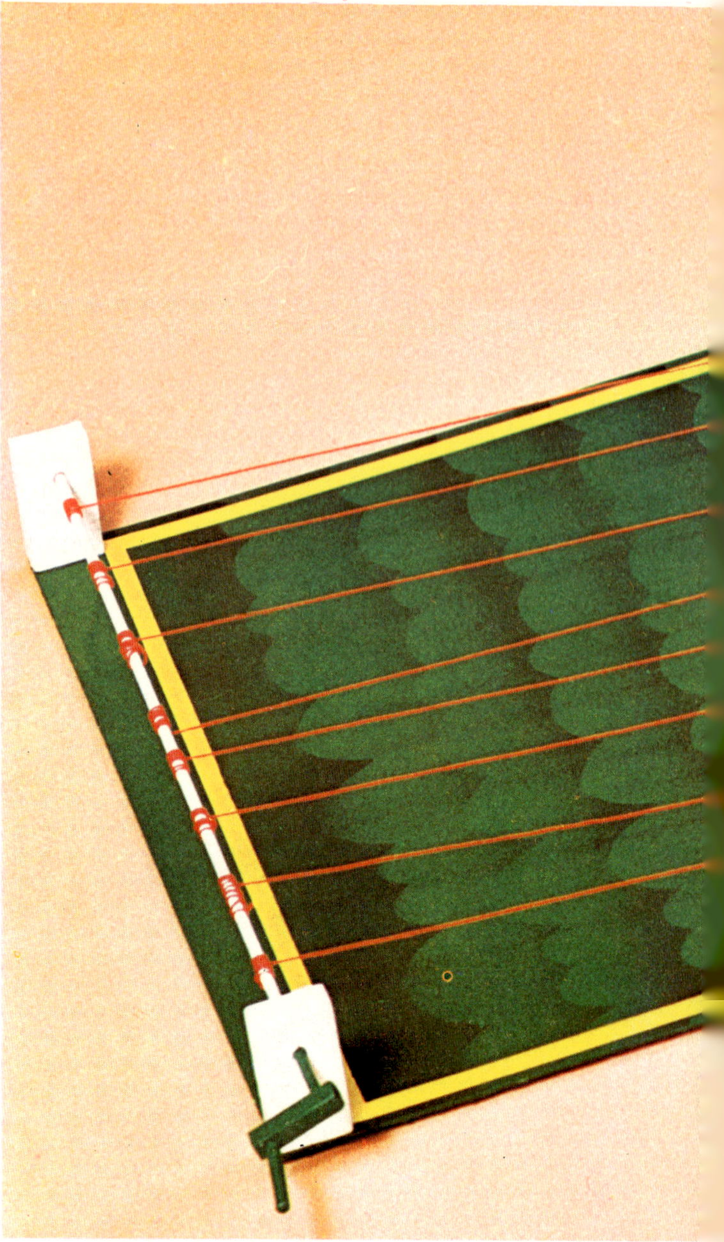

4 For the finishing line:
Drill a hole for the dowel in the uprights.
Make a turning handle as shown.
Fix the finishing post to the track.
Stand the horses in line at the starting post. Tie strings from their staples to the finishing post.
Turn the handle and the horses are off!

CHINESE CHEQUERS

You will need:

large piece of heavy card
pencil ruler glue
paints and paint brush
36 corks
bottle tops

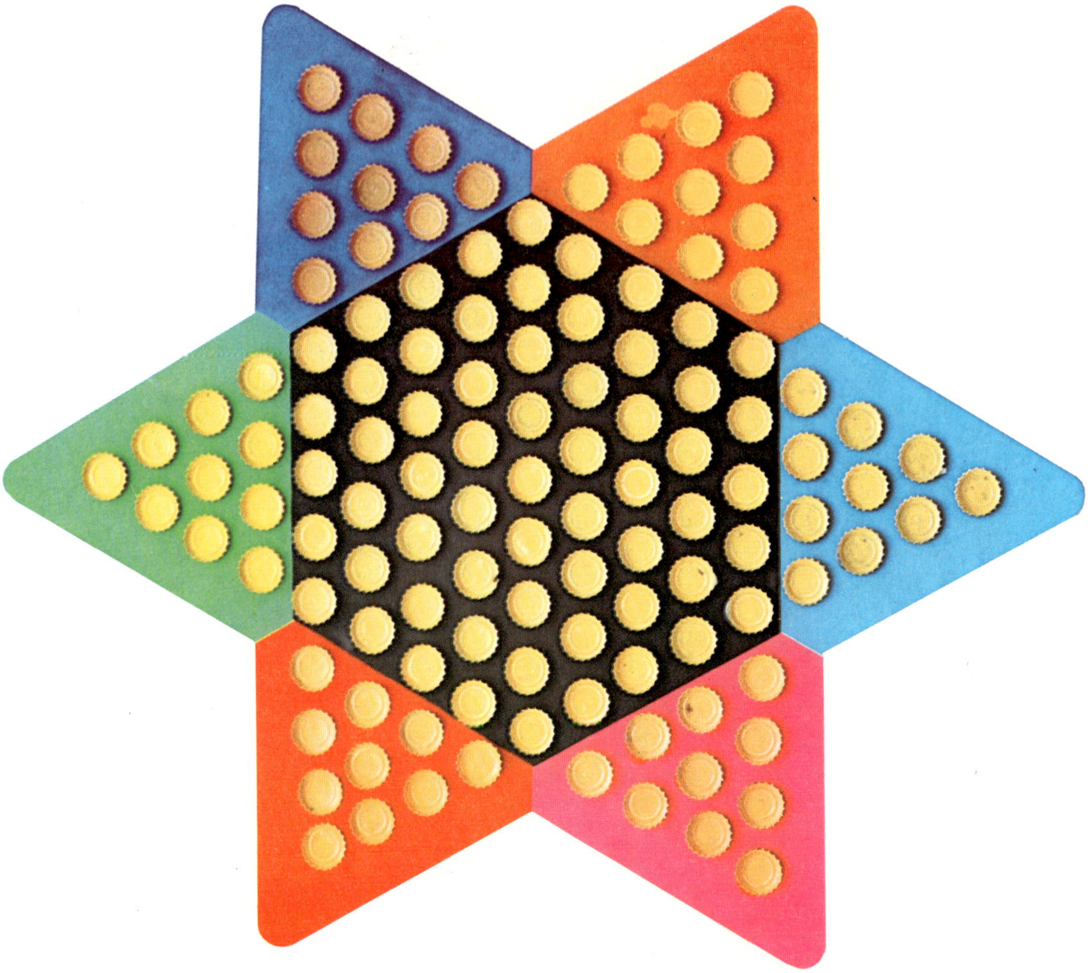

1 On the card rule out the design of the Chinese Chequers board.

2 Cut out the board.
Paint the sections in bright colours of your own choice.

3 Glue the bottle tops onto the card as shown in the diagram, starting at the tip of each star.
Paint the insides of the bottle tops.

4 Paint the corks in the same colours as the side sections of the board (six for each section).
Your game is now ready to play.
The instructions for playing the game are as follows:

The object of the game is to move your corks to the point of the star opposite to where you began. Whoever does this first is the winner.

1 Each player puts her coloured corks into a point of the star.

2 Each player takes a turn to move a cork in any direction. You can move one hole or can jump as many corks as you like so long as they are successive.

3 You can jump over your own corks as well as another player's. No corks are removed from the board.

MAGNETIC SPINNER

You will need:

sheet of plywood
3 long nails
length of 12.5 mm balsa
6 small magnets
3 bottle tops
saw   drill

1 Cut an equilateral triangle from the plywood.

2 Drill a small hole at the tip of each of the points in the triangle. Fix a nail point upwards in each hole. These should be firmly fixed in order to support the balsa wood arms.

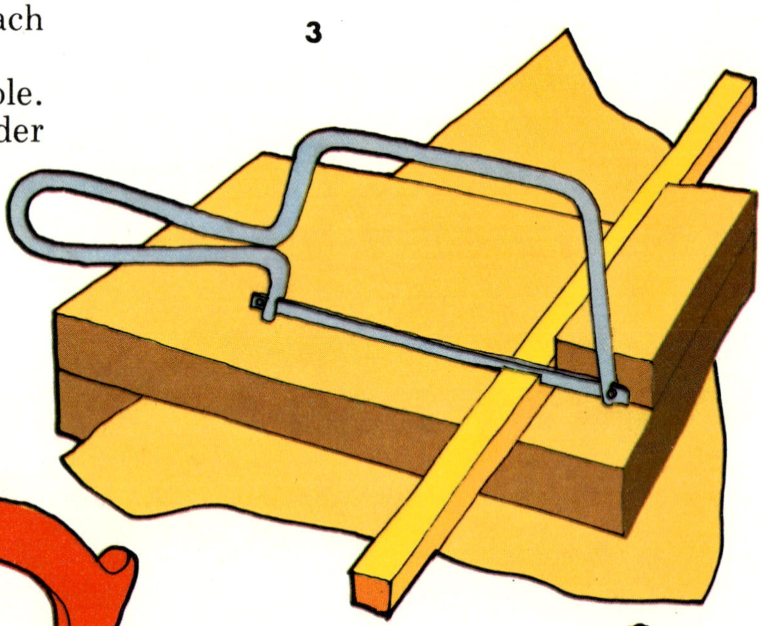

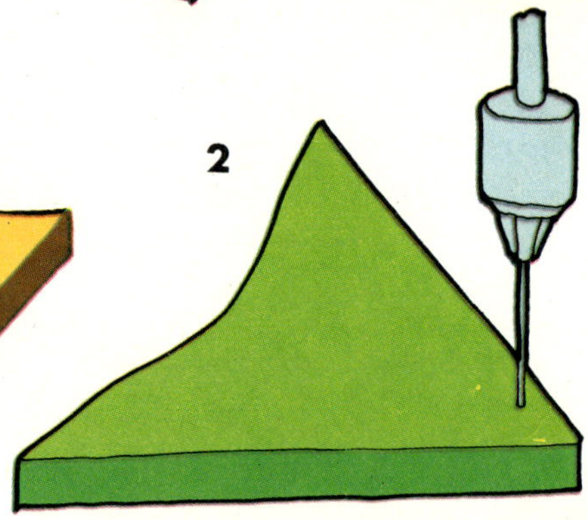

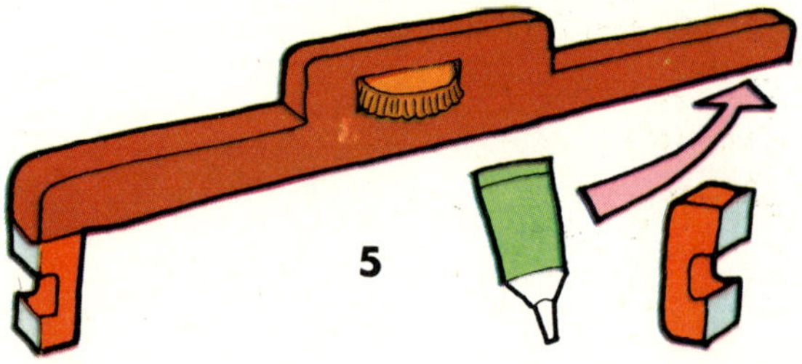

3 Cut 3 lengths of balsa long enough so that if they are fixed at their centres on the nails, they will miss each other by about 3 cm when they spin.

4 Find the centre of each length and drill a small hole.
Remove the cork layer from the bottle tops.
Fix each of the bottle tops over the drilled hole with lengths of balsa, making sure that they are glued firmly into position. Gently tap an impression on to the bottle tops with a nail to act as pivot points.

5 Glue a magnet on to the ends of each arm.
Different effects will depend on whether the magnets are fixed to repel or attract each other. Carefully, balance the 3 arms on the 3 nails in the triangular base.
Spin the arms round and see what happens.

BUILDING SET

You will need:

lengths of 28 × 28 mm pine
dowel rod
saw vice drill
sandpaper
paints and paint brush

1 Saw the lengths of pine into cubes.

2 Hold the cubes in your vice and drill holes the diameter of the dowel rod through from each side.

3 Cut the dowel rod into a number of varying lengths.

4 Sand off the corners and surfaces of the cubes. Paint the cubes and rods in bright colours.

With the construction kit that you have now made you can build all manner of machines, robots and animals. You can add to your kit whenever you need to and you can invent different shaped pieces to suit any model.

TRIANGULAR STACKING BRICKS

You will need:

card
cutting tool
coloured papers
sticky tape

1

2

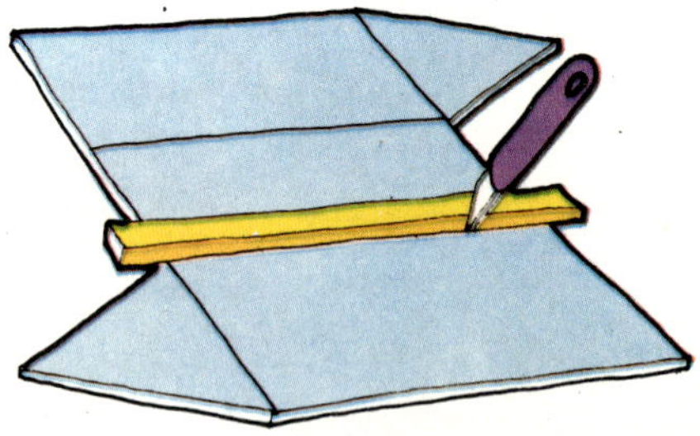

3

4

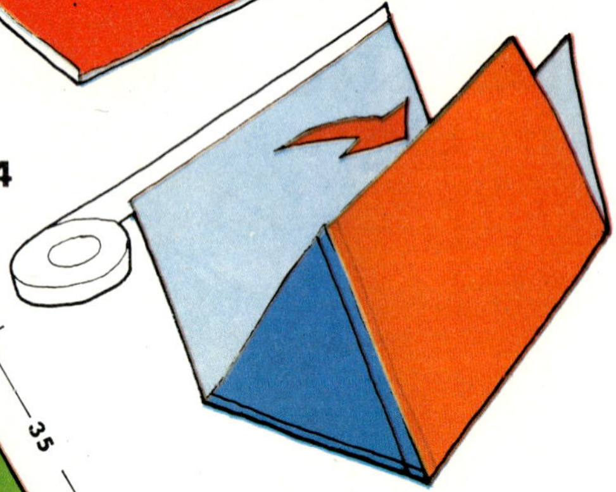

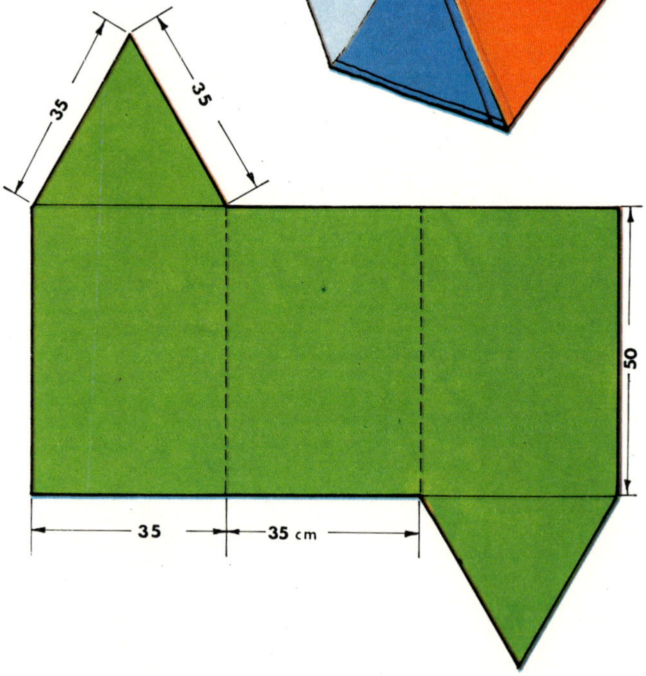

1 Cut out the card to the size you want as shown in the diagram.

2 Score the folds gently.

3 Cut out different coloured papers to cover the different sections of one side of the cut out card.

4 Bend the card up along the fold lines.
Tape the sides together to form the triangular shape.

5 When you have made a number of these bricks in contrasting colours, them into each other or stack them together to decorate your room. You can move them around whenever you wish to form different combinations and patterns.

WOOL ANIMALS

You will need:

wool
knitting needles (size 7)
felt stuffing
needle and thread
scissors

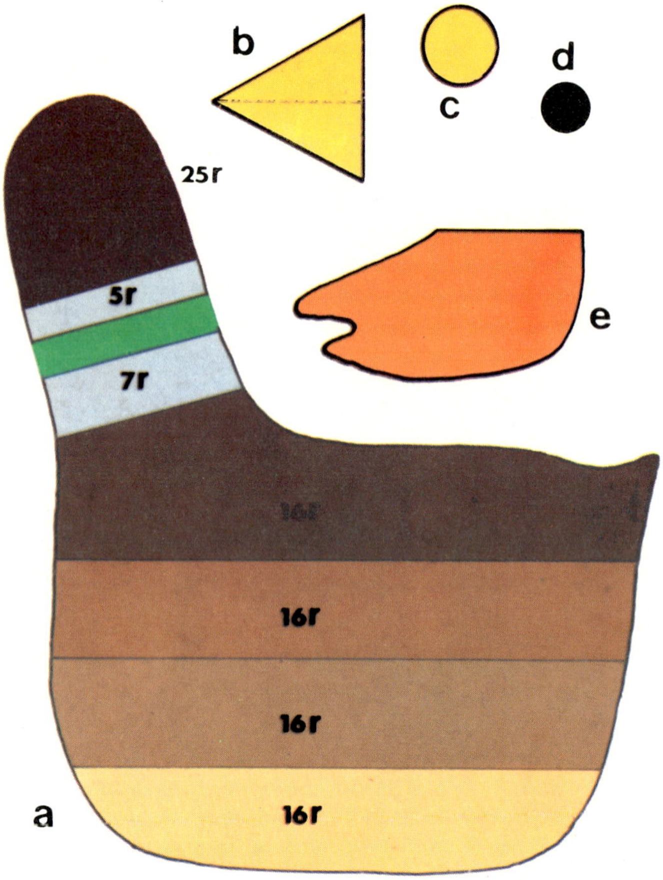

Mouse
You need brown and grey wool, which you twine together as you knit.
Cast on 80 stitches. Knit 5 rows. Decrease 1 stitch at each end of next 60 rows. Cast off remaining 20 stitches. Knit the other side exactly the same. Sew the two sides together, leaving an opening for the stuffing. Stuff the body. Cut tail, ears and eyes in felt. Sew them in place.

Duck
You need black, light blue, green, dark brown, mid-brown, light brown and white wool.
Cast on 60 stitches in white. Knit 16 rows. Change to light brown. Increase 1 stitch at start of next 6 rows. Knit 10 rows. Change to mid-brown. Increase

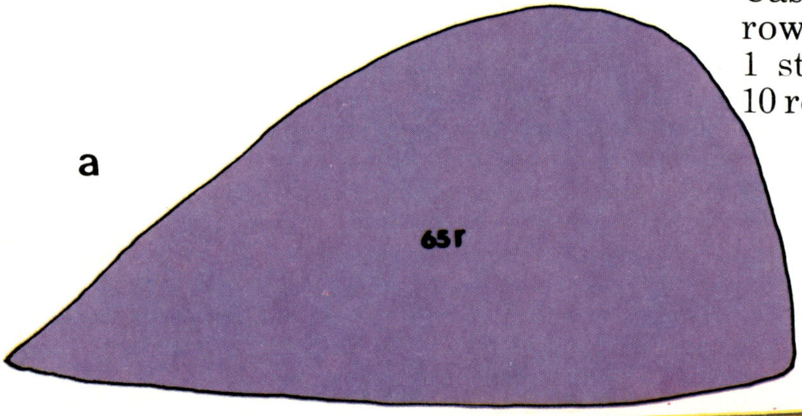

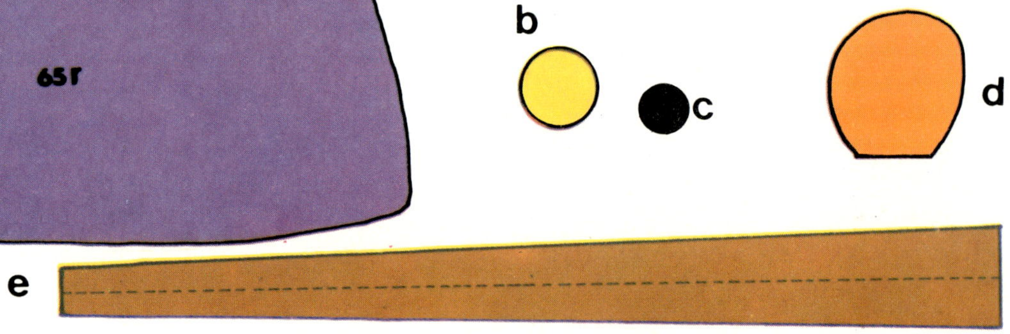

1 stitch at start of next 6 rows. Knit 10 rows. Change to dark brown. Increase 1 stitch at start of next 6 rows. Knit 10 rows. Cast off 50 stitches. (10 stitches.) Change to blue. Knit 7 rows. Change to green. Knit 6 rows. Change to black. Knit 25 rows. Cast off. Knit the other side exactly the same. Sew the sides together. Shape the head while you are sewing it up. Stuff the body of the duck. Make sure the stuffing in the neck is firm. Cut pieces of felt for feet, beak and eyes. Sew them on to the body.

Fish

You need pink, red and purple wool. Cast on 10 stitches in pink. Knit 1 row. Increase 1 stitch at start of each row for 44 rows. Change to red. Knit 12 rows increasing 1 stitch at start of each row. Change to purple. Knit 12 rows increasing 1 stitch at start of each row. (78 stitches.) Change to pink. Knit 12 rows decreasing 1 stitch at start of each row. Change to red. Knit 16 rows decreasing 1 stitch at start of each row. Change to purple. Knit 16 rows decreasing 1 stitch at start of each row. Change to pink. Knit 12 rows decreasing at both ends of each row until 10 stitches remain. Cast off. Knit the other side exactly the same. Sew the sides together. Stuff the body. Cut pieces of felt for fins and eyes. Sew them on to the body of the fish.

a

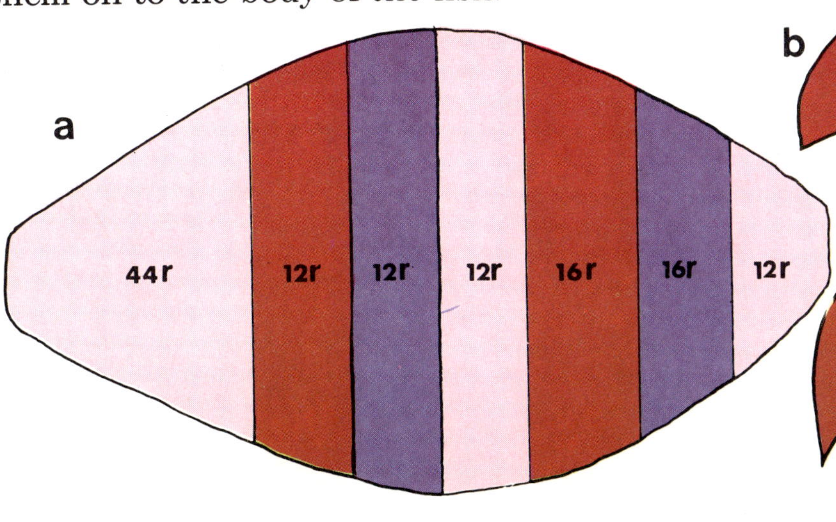

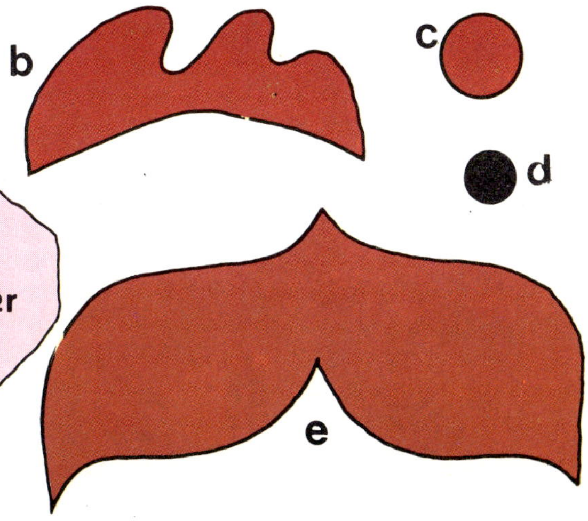

HARP

You will need:

old picture frame
piece of plywood saw
ruler pencil glue
paints and paint brushes
30 eyelets nylon guitar strings

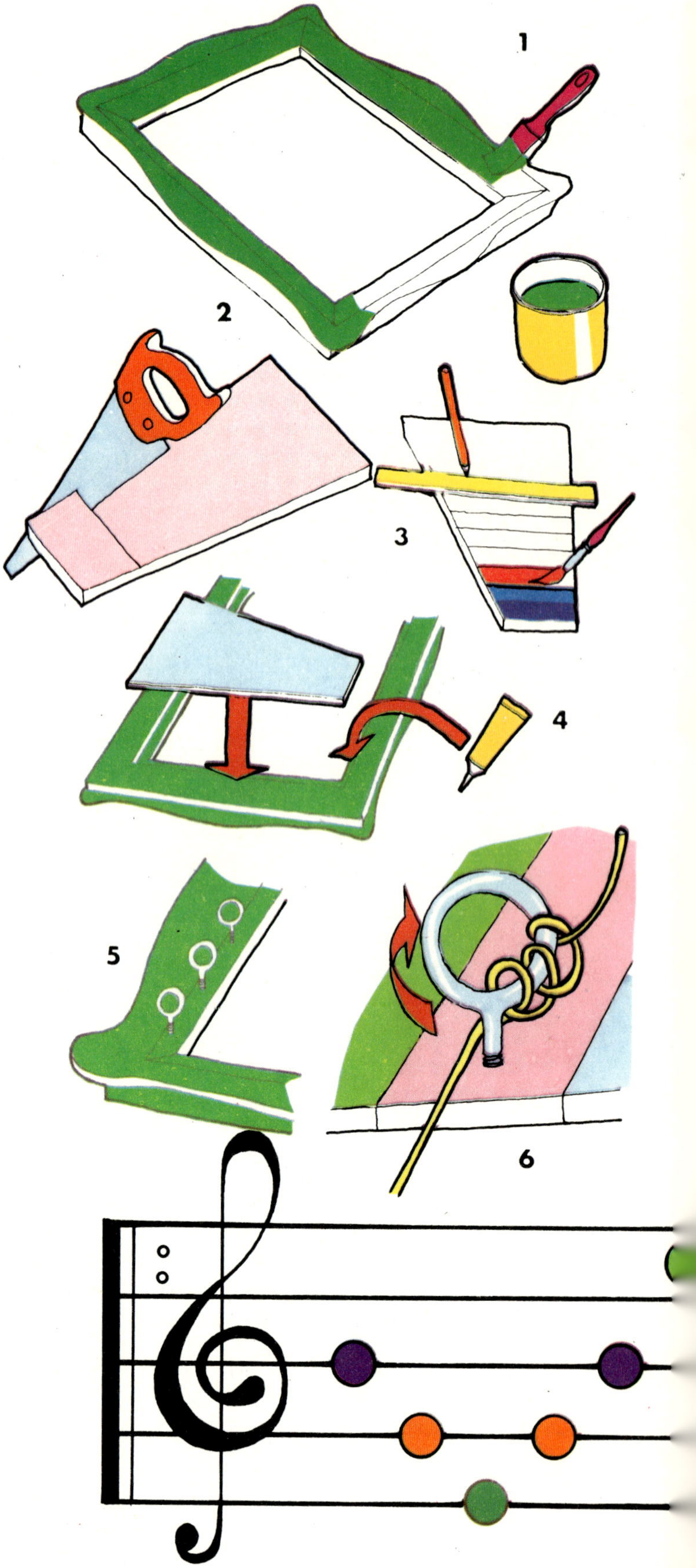

1 Clean and paint the picture frame.

2 Cut the piece of plywood so that it fits exactly into the back of the frame. One end is wider than the other to make the strings longer at one end than the other to give bass and treble notes.

3 Rule the piece of plywood into 15 equal divisions. Paint each division following the colours on the diagram. Each division is a different note. The 15 divisions will give you two octaves or two major scales: doh reh me fah so la te doh, and back again.

4 Glue the note board to the frame. Allow the glue to set firmly.

5 Screw 15 eyelets into the top of the frame equi-distant apart. Screw 15 eyelets onto the note board centred in each colour division.

6 Attach the guitar strings to the eyelets. Use base (thick) strings for the low (short) notes and treble (thin) strings for the high (long) notes.

7 Tune your harp by ear or with a piano. Now play this famous piece of music and try writing your own pieces of music using coloured notes.

Buzz, Buzz, Buzz

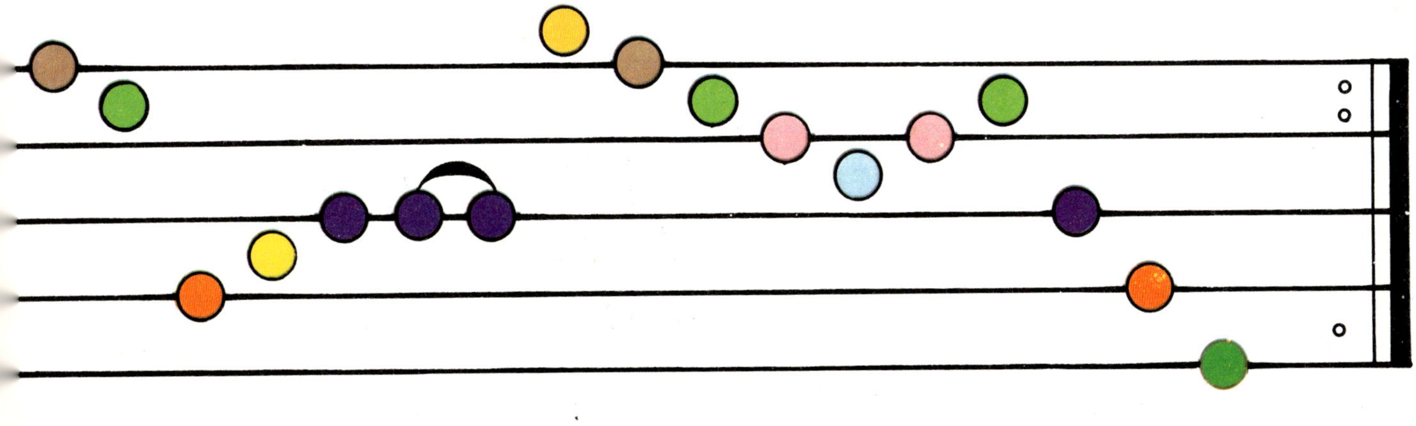

CHIMES

You will need:

lengths of 12.5 × 12.5 mm wood
a sheet of light plywood
3 metres 12.5 mm right angled
aluminium edging
nylon line   hooks or drawing pins
drill   wood and metal saws
paint and paint brush
glue

1 Cut 5 lengths of wood 68 cm (A) and 1 length 86 cm (B). Cut the ends at angles.

2 Cut 8 lengths of edging (approximately 55, 50, 45, 35, 30, 22, 15 and 8 cm long).

3 Form 2 triangles at right angles to each other with the A lengths. Fix the B length from tip to tip of the triangles to form the frame. Starting 4 cm from the top end of B, drill 8 holes 4 cm apart. Form the base with plywood and glue the frame on.

4 Drill holes at top and bottom of the edging. Suspend the pieces with nylon line to B and give 4 cm clearance top and bottom. Fix to base with hooks or pins and line. Paint the base in 8 coloured lines for the notes. Tap your tunes with another length of edging.

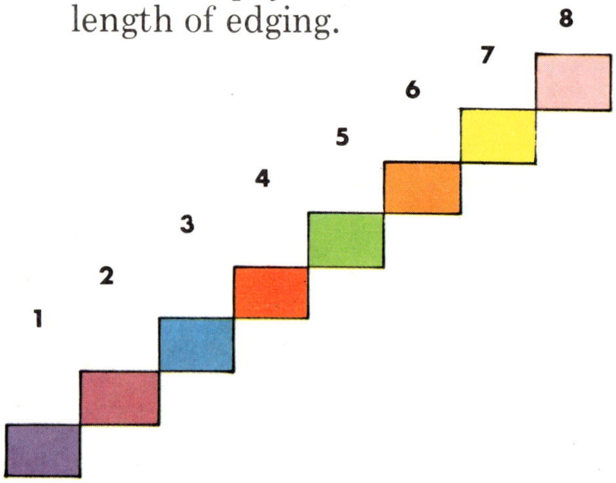

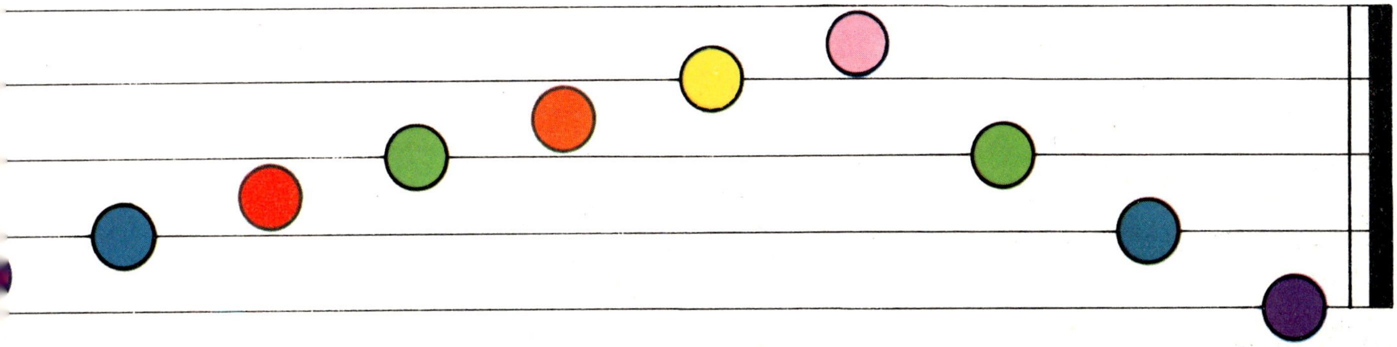

TOY BOX CAR

You will need:

sheets of 12.5 mm chipboard
blocks and pieces of wood
saw   screwdriver   4 hinges
screws   nails   hammer
sandpaper   paint   brush

1 Measure and cut out the sheets of chipboard as shown. Cut two of piece A and one each of the others. Make the main box shape with pieces A, B, C and F. Fix pieces D and E on with hinges to form the seat and lid as shown in 2.

2 Fix a piece of wood on to the left side for the seat to rest on. Fix a piece of wood on to the right side to support the lid.

3 Fix a block under the rear end of the lid. Screw on steering wheel.

4 Fit the windscreen. Sand all edges and paint the car with a white undercoat. Decorate it. Add door handles and tin lids for lights.

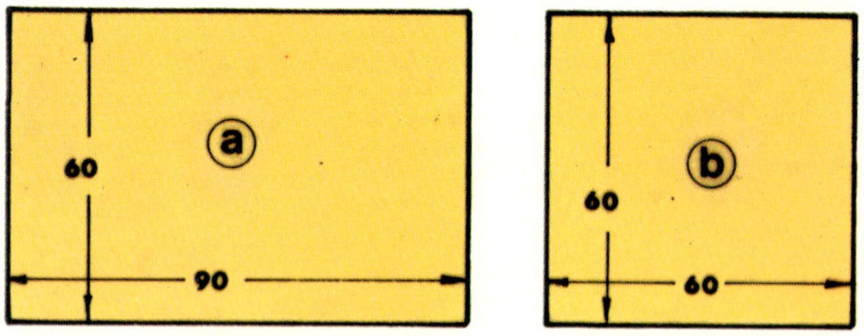

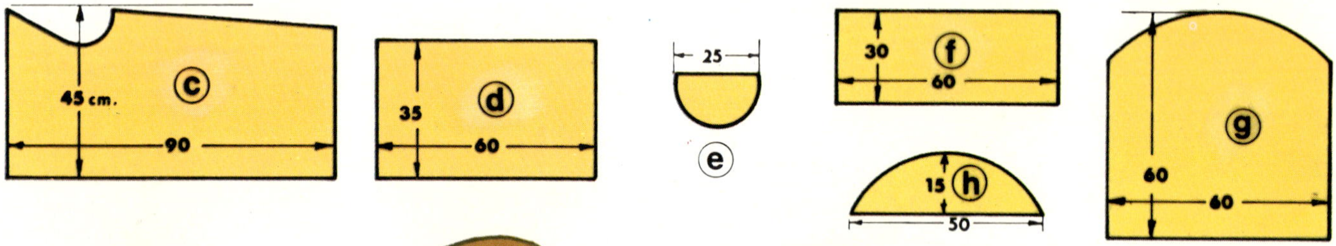

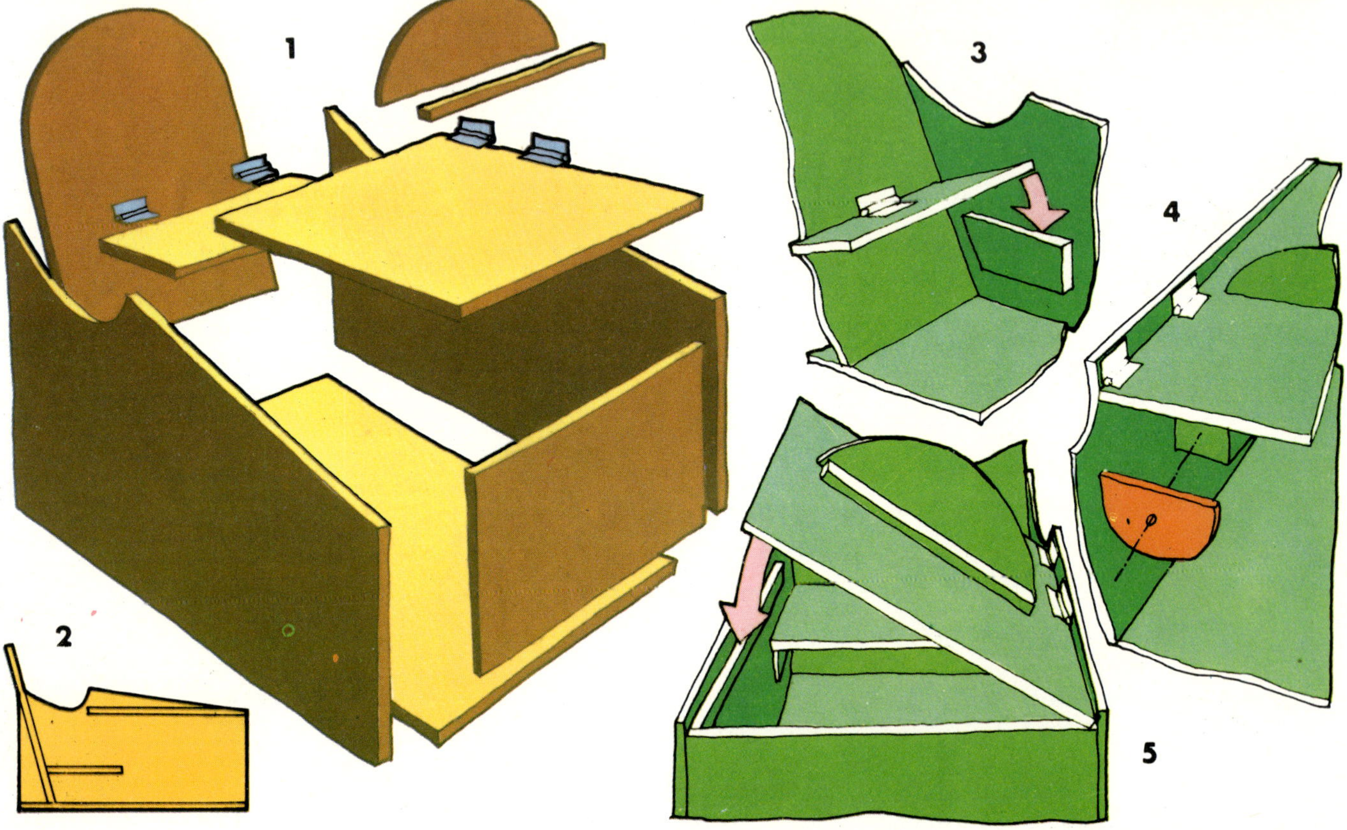

PLAY FAMILY HOUSE

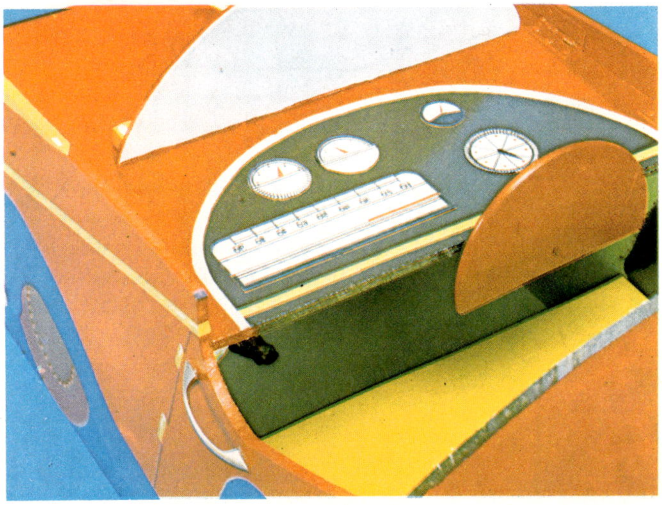

PICTURE MAKING

CLOTHES PEG ART

You will need:

clothes pegs
heavy card or sheet of wood
glue   drinking straws
paints and paint brush

You can use a mixture of wooden and plastic pegs or you can make your picture out of one sort of peg.

1 Take the clothes pegs to pieces. Paint some of them if you wish.

2 Paint the piece of card or board and let it dry thoroughly.
Compose a picture on this base with the clothes pegs. Add drinking straws, drawing pins or any other suitable materials. Use the spring clips from the pegs in your composition too.
When you are satisfied with your composition, glue each peg down in position.

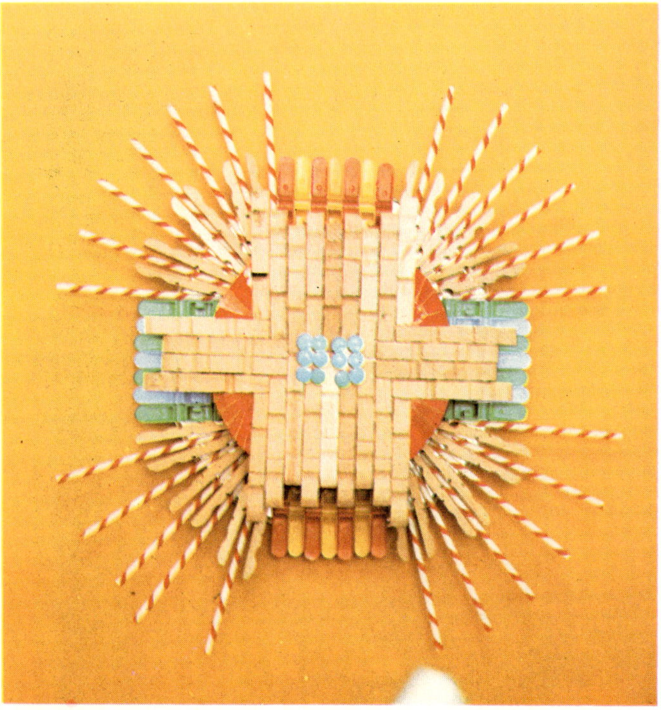

1

2

SHELL PICTURES

You will need:

heavy coloured cards
shells thread
glue
cutting tool
coloured tape

1 Collect together an assortment of shells which give you a variety of shapes, colours and textures.

2 Arrange your shells into a picture of flowers and leaves on a piece of card. Use coloured thread for the stalks.

3 When you are satisfied with the arrangement, glue it onto the card.

4 Take another piece of coloured card the same size as the base. Rule a line 3 cm from the edge all the way round. Cut the centre panel out. Glue the remaining frame to the base. You can decorate the frame with coloured tape.

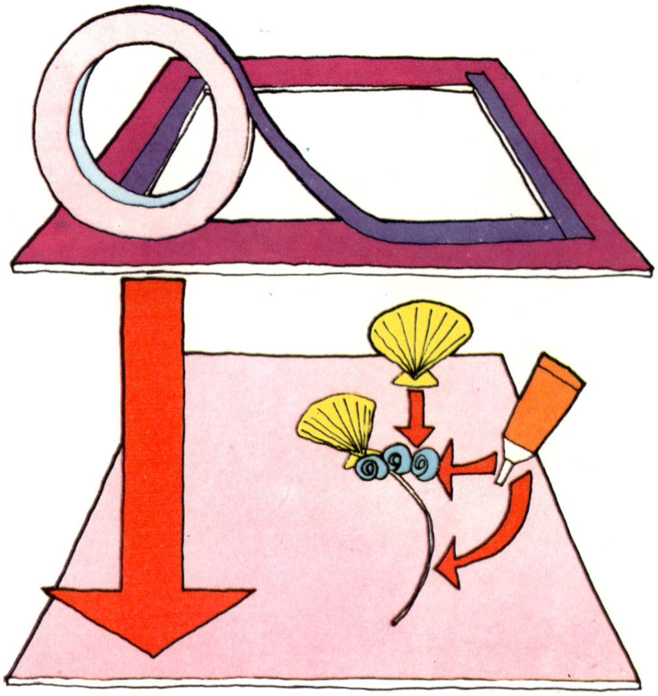

PRESSED FLOWERS

You will need:

piece of paper
a heavy book
light card
glue   cutting tool
thread

1 Collect flowers, leaves and grass. As soon as possible place them in paper inside a heavy book. Leave them for at least 3 weeks – the longer the better. Take a piece of card and make a composition with the dried flowers on it. When you are satisfied with the arrangement, glue it down.

2 To frame your picture, cut out strips of card and glue them round it.

3 Another sort of frame can be made by cutting a circle or other shape from contrasting coloured card and gluing it down around your picture.

4 You can make a very delicate frame by binding thread round the card and tying it behind.
Glue piece of backing card to the back of the picture to hide the knots.

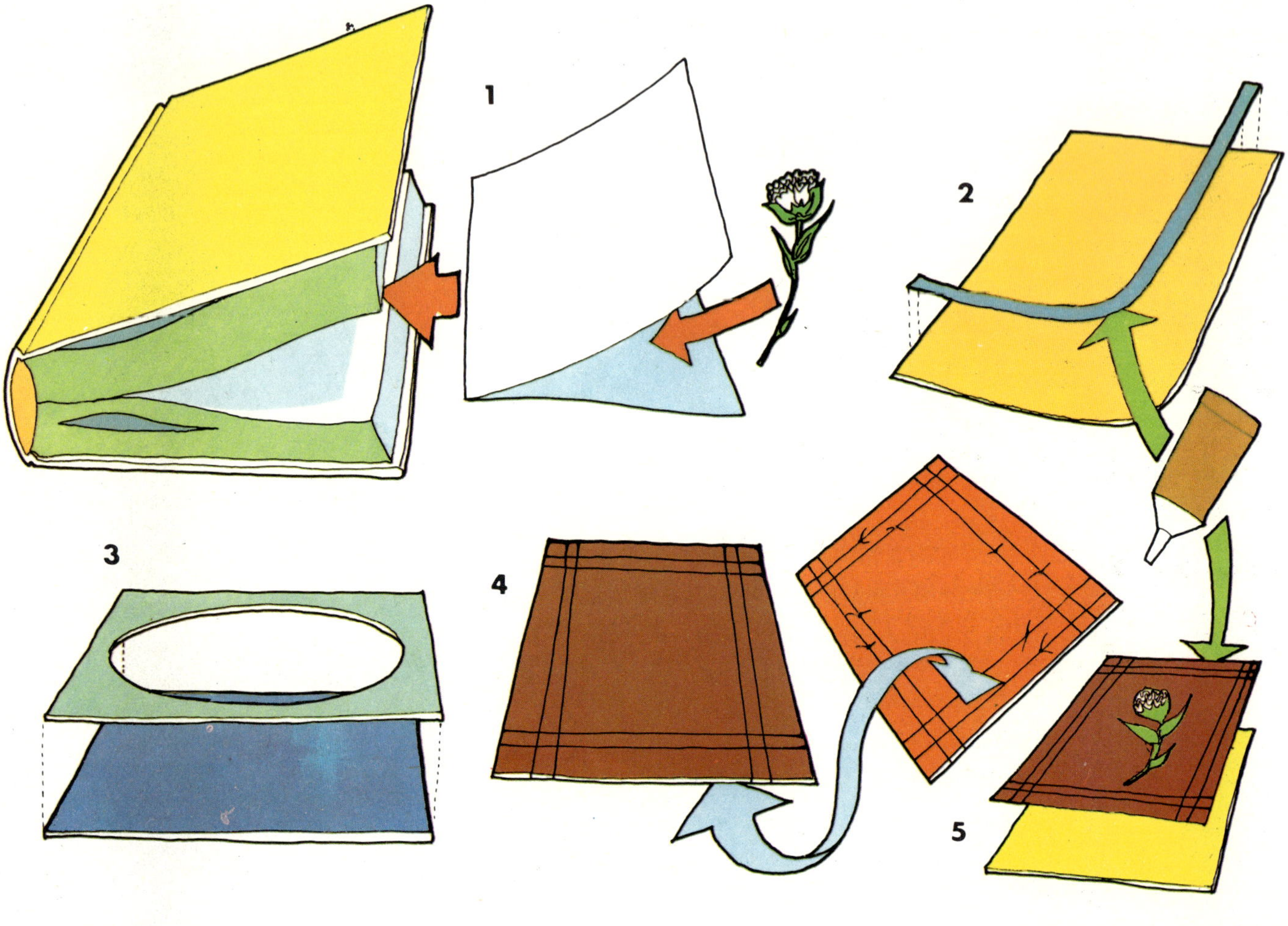

POP UP PICTURES

You will need:

card light paper
scoring tool
scissors
glue
paint and paint brush

Ballooning

1 Cut the background shape to the size you want. Score along the dotted lines. Fold down on the strong lines and up on the weak lines. Colour the card.

2 Glue on the flowers and clouds. Draw in a figure floating on the balloon.

Delicious Cake

1 Cut and fold the backing card.

2 Cut the see-through shape from light paper. Glue to the backing card.

3 Cut out 4 cake sections. Fold at the centres and edges. Decorate with

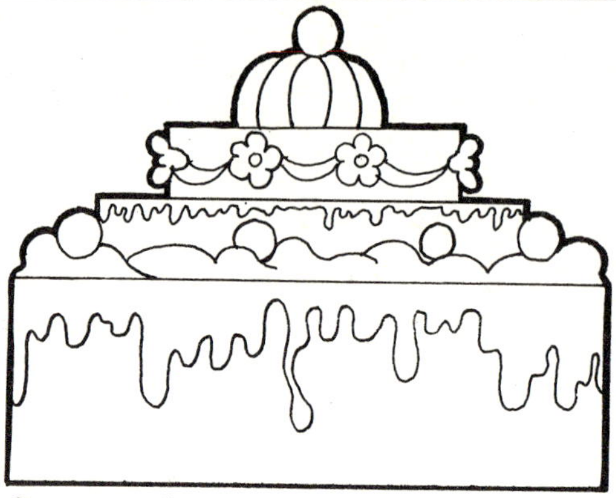

paint and paper. Flatten out the backing card and cake sections. Align the centre folds. Glue the edges to the backing card, starting with the inner section.

Valentine

Cut out the backing card. Cut out the heart with side flaps. Cut a window in the heart. Take your picture and fold down the edges. Glue the edges to the back of the heart so the face looks through the window. Glue the heart on to the backing card.

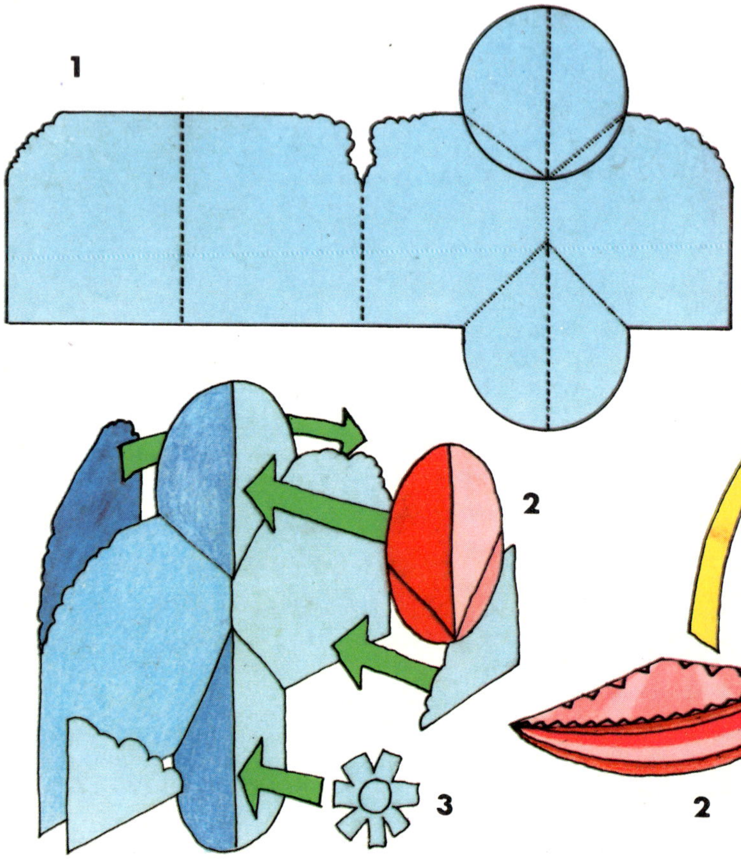

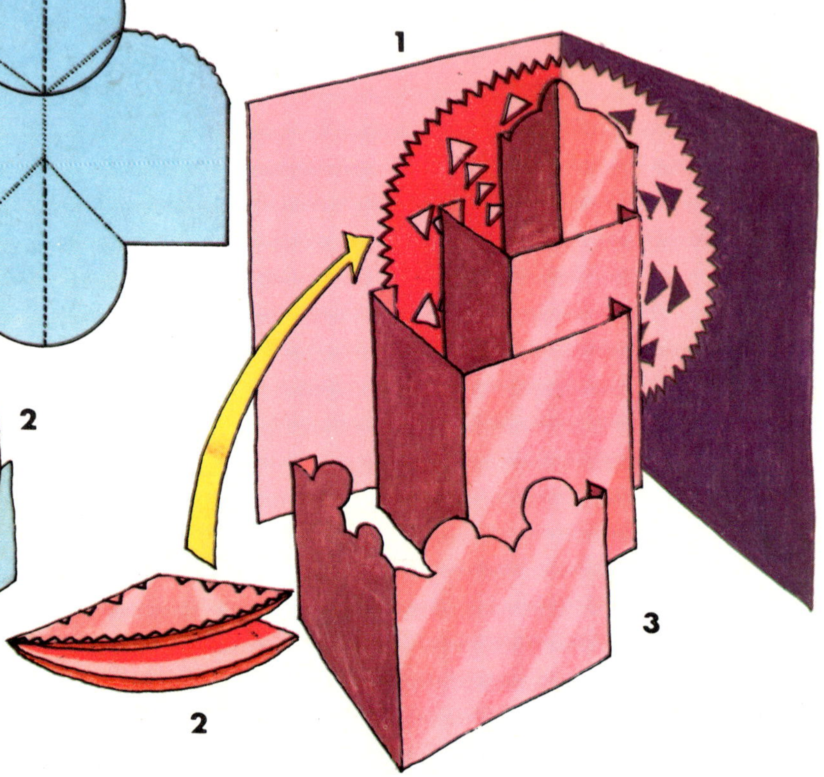

PICTURE STORAGE UNIT

You will need:

cardboard box
cardboard tubes
coloured card
cutting tool
glue   pencil
paint and paint brush

It is often very difficult to find somewhere to store your posters, paintings and other big sheets of paper where they will not get torn and dog-eared. This unit will answer the problem.

1 Cut the flaps away at the top and bottom of the box.

2 Glue the coloured card onto the outside of the box.

3 Draw the diameter of each tube on both sides of the box.

4 Cut these circles out carefully.

5 Paint the tubes. Push them through the holes in the box.
Store your posters in the tubes.

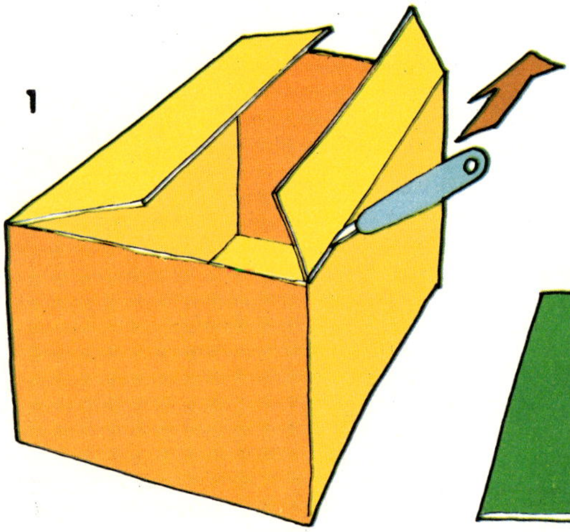

3

4

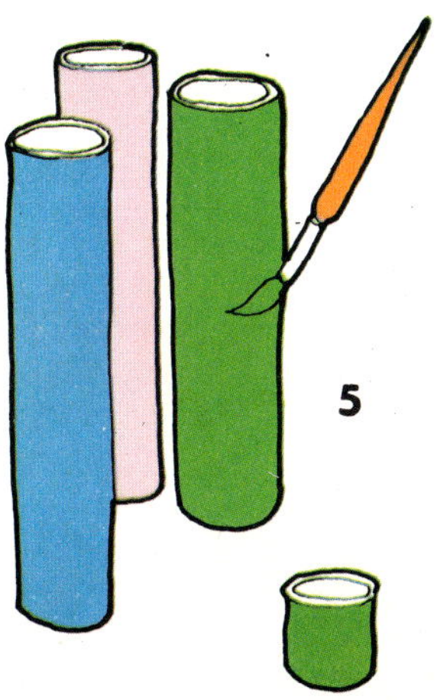

5

PLAYING WITH PLANTS

JAPANESE GARDEN

You will need:

lengths and sheet of wood
hammer nails glue
paint paint brush tape
Japanese fibre paper
pebbles soft wire red card

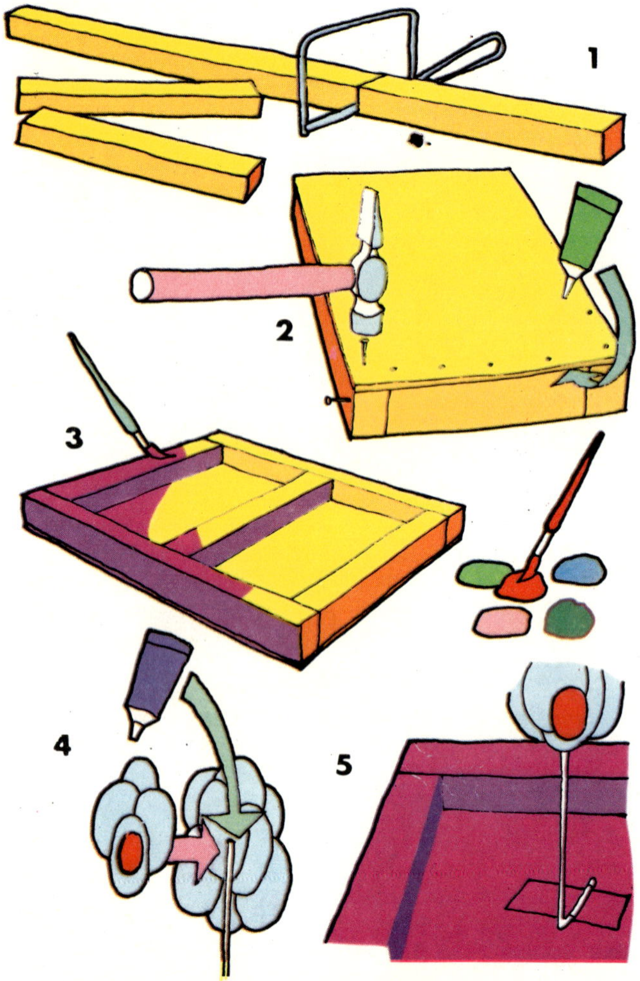

1 Cut two 50 cm lengths of wood (3·5 × 3·5 cm) and three 23 cm lengths. Nail 1 short bit in the centre of the 2 long bits like an H.
Nail 2 short lengths in the ends of the H.

2 Nail a sheet of wood 50 cm × 30 cm to this frame.

3 Paint the box you have made.
Paint half your pebbles with enamel paints.

4 Cut paper disks 6 cm in diameter. Cut lengths of wire about 35 cm long. Glue 3 or 4 disks to each wire, finishing off with a disk of red card.

5 Bend the ends of the wire. Tape them to the bottom of the box. Put the stones in the box.

FLORAL UMBRELLA

You will need:

a transparent umbrella
crêpe paper
scissors
wool string

1 Cut crêpe paper into strips about 10 cm wide and 40 cm long. Cut curves along one edge. Start with half a dozen curves and then try varying the number, shape and size of the curves to see what sort of flowers different shapes will make.

2 Curl the paper into a loose roll. Squeeze the lower edge together quite tightly and bind it with wool. Leave a generous length of wool on some of the flowers.

You will need to make about 50–60 flowers to fill the average umbrella. Suspend the umbrella from a string. Fill it with flowers. Suspend some flowers from the lengths of wool round the spokes of the umbrella.

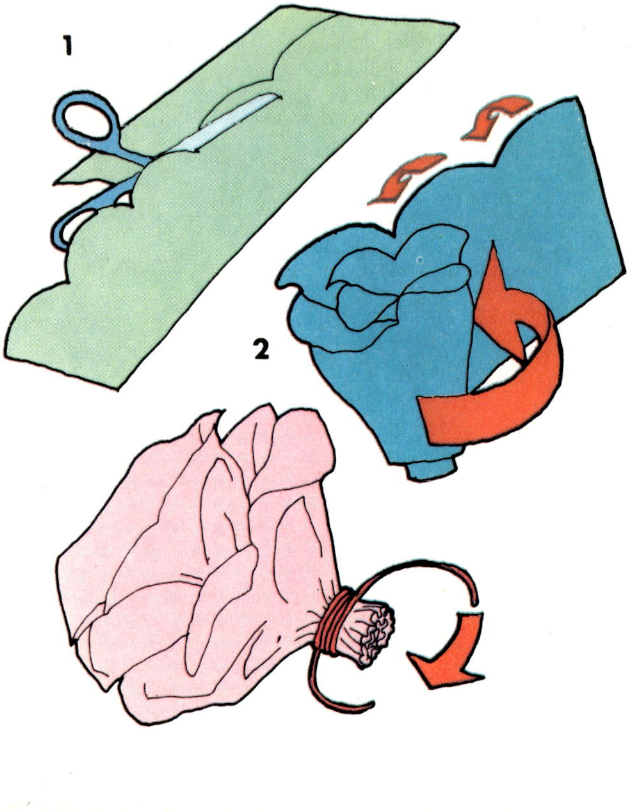

CLOCK FLOWERS

You will need:

an old alarm clock
soft wire   pliers
scouring powder tin
paint and paint brush

You need pieces from old alarm clocks to make these flowers – so it is not something you can make every day. A charity shop or sale might be your best source of supply.

Unscrew all the parts and salvage the most interesting shapes.

1 Using pliers, bend lengths of wire 30–40 cm long tightly around the spindles and centres of the cogs.

2 Paint the scouring powder tin.

Arrange your clock flowers through the perforations in the top of your scouring powder flower vase.

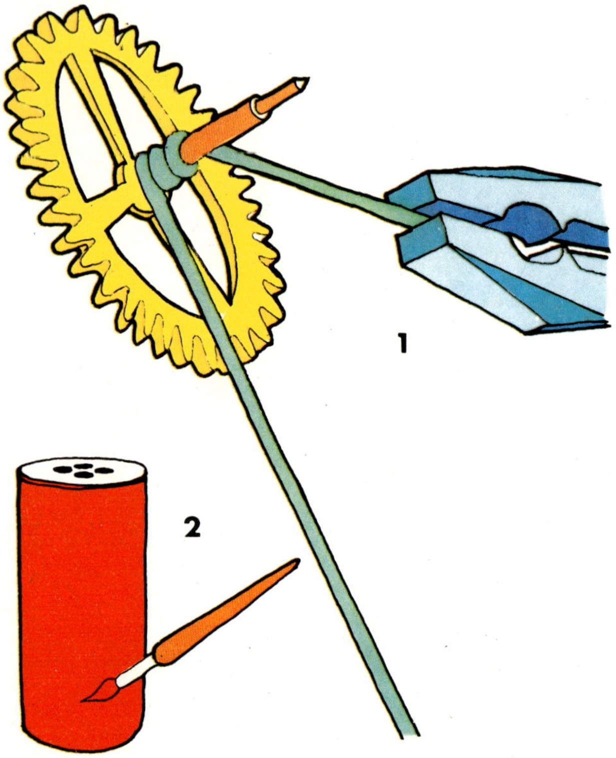

PLANT POTS

You will need:

containers
paint and paint brush
glue   coloured tape
cutting tool   card
paint spray

You can make plant pots from any clean, water tight container in which you can make drainage holes.

1 This dog is made from a detergent bottle. Cut an opening. Decorate with tape and paint. Use lids for legs and card for ears.

2 Brighten up ordinary flower pots with coloured tape and paint.

3 Convert a detergent bottle, plastic cups and card into a lady.

4 Cut cylinders from plastic bottles. Link them with a card rainbow.

5 Spray stencil patterns onto an old bucket or paint can.

CRESS GARDEN

You will need:

plant pot
cotton wool
absorbent tissue
mustard and cress seeds
watering can

1 Take one of the plant pots you have made. Fill it to within 2 cm of the top with cotton wool. Cover this with 6 layers of tissue.

2 Dampen the tissue with water.

3 Sprinkle cress seeds onto the damp surface. Put the pot near a window in a warm room. Four days later dampen the tissue again and sprinkle on the mustard seeds. Mustard grows faster than cress.

When the cress is about 5 cm high and the mustard about 8 cm high, harvest your crop and eat it in sandwiches.

PLANT WRITING

You will need:

wood nails
hammer saw
drill
soil stones
mustard seeds

1 Make a wooden box approximately 20 × 30 × 5 cm in size.

2 Drill some holes in the bottom.

3 Turn the box over and put a layer of small stones in the bottom. This will encourage good drainage.
Stand the box in a tray to catch drips. Paint the box if you wish.

4 Fill the box to within about 1 cm of the top with soil.
Smooth down the soil with a small piece of wood about 1·5 cm wide and make an impression about 5 mm deep of the letters of your name in the soil.
Fill these grooves with mustard seeds. Cover the seeds with a light layer of soil. Sprinkle water on the seed box.
Place the box in a light, warm place . . . and wait.

1

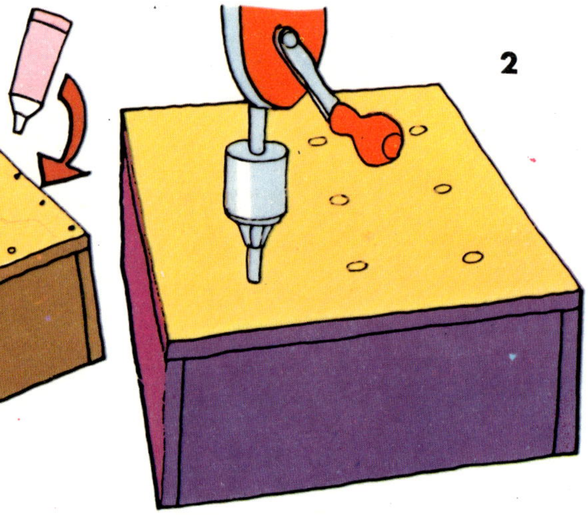

2

3

4

MINIATURE GARDEN

You will need:

large container
drill
pebbles
sand
compost
small glass bowl
cacti
modelling clay
paint
paint brush

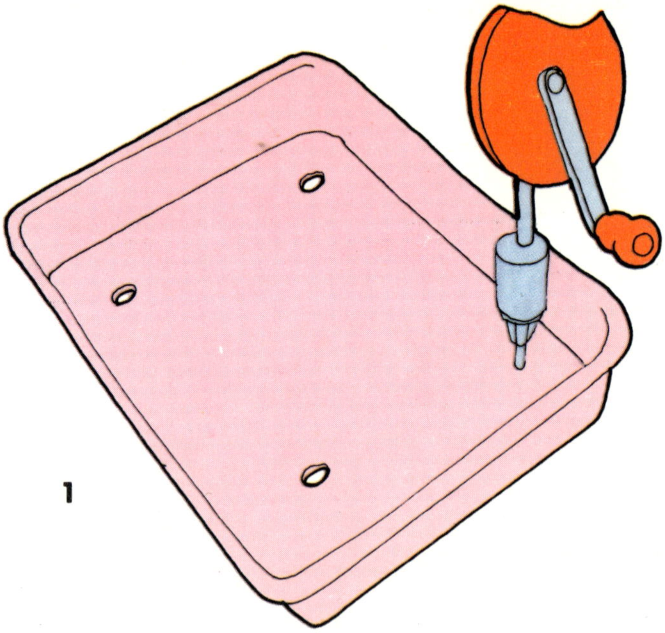

1

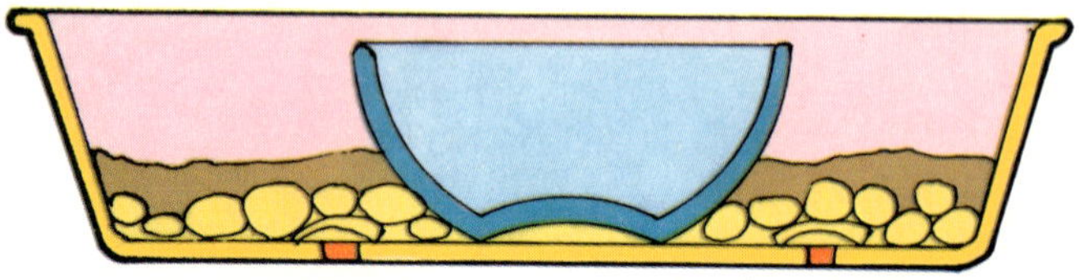

2

3

4

1 Take a container with holes in the base so that any excess water can drain through.
If the container has no holes, drill one hole in each corner.

2 Line the bottom of the container with small pebbles. Cover the pebbles with a mixture of washed sand and compost.
Sink a small glass bowl into the soil which will act as a pond. Conceal the lip of the bowl with small pebbles.

3 Cacti can be bought from a gardening store or a flower shop.
If, however, you want to grow your own, plant the seeds in a pot, cover with foil and leave in a warm place. It is sufficient to water them every 3 or 4 days. When they are grown, separate them carefully, ease them out of the pot and transfer them to your miniature garden.

4 You can make miniature castles, houses and any other decorations you might want out of modelling clay.
Paint small pebbles in different colours to brighten up your garden.

PLANTS AS GIFTS

You will need:

The materials you need are given in the instructions.

Dried flower plant

1 Tape dried flower heads onto a wire stem to create a new type of plant.
2 Arrange other flower heads according to their colour.
3 Stand the flowers in a bowl of sand.

Underwater garden

You can buy underwater plants from any fish or aquarium supplier. They also sell gravel and sometimes recommend special soil.

1 Take a large bottle or jar. Put gravel in it.
2 Compose the plants in a satisfactory arrangement on the bottom.
3 Put the rocks in last.

Glue cellophane fish to the outside of the container if you wish.

Flowering branch

1 Paint a branch in a bright colour.
2 Fix dried or freshly picked flower heads onto the branch with tape.
3 Glue it into a circle of cork or polystyrene. Fix it in a lid.

DISPLAYING THINGS

SHELL FISH

You will need:

card
paint and paint brush
cutting tool
tube 8 cm diameter
glue

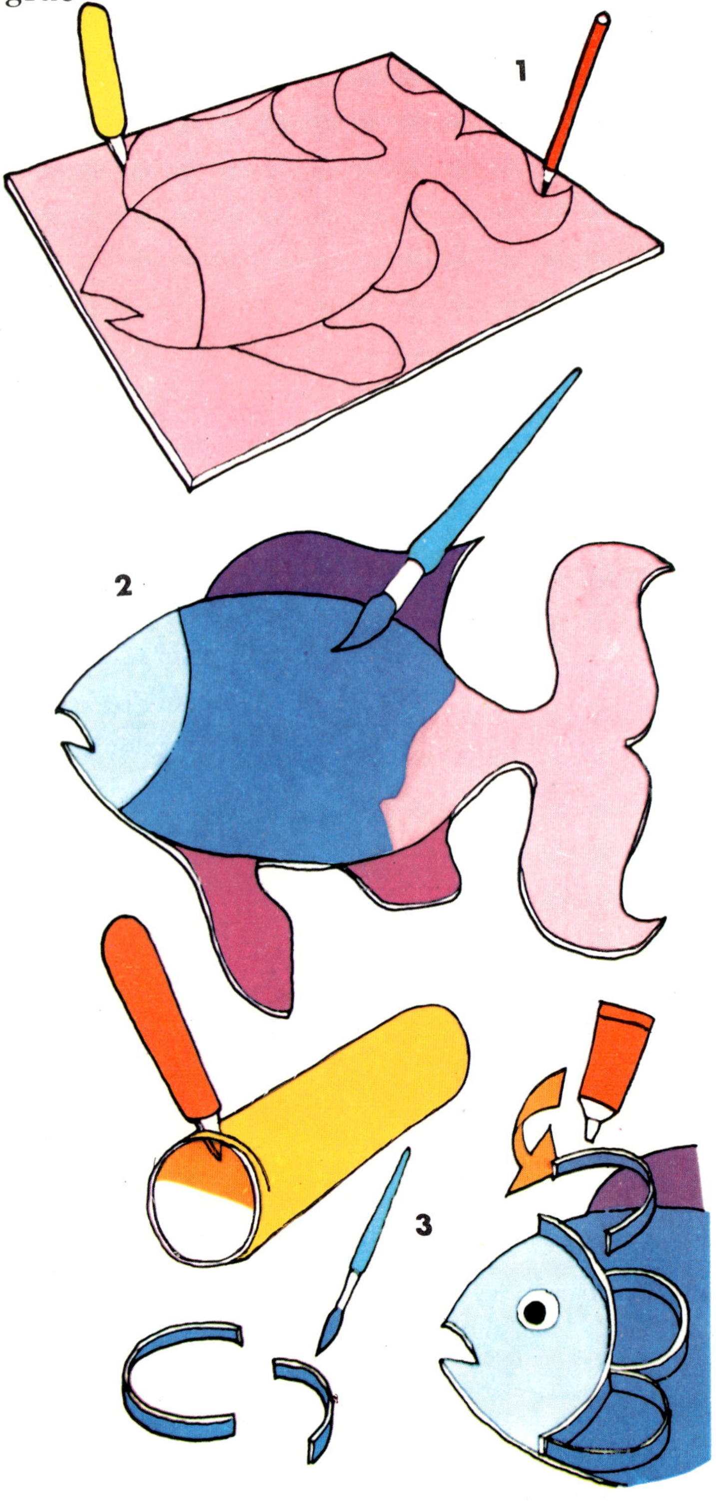

1 Draw the fish onto the card.

2 Cut it out and paint it.

3 Cut rings 1·5 cm wide from the tube. Cut a third off each ring. Paint the remainder. Cut a card 1·5 cm wide, long enough to curve round the fish's head. Glue these curved pieces in position. Glue on shells.

DISPLAY WHEEL

You will need:

compass heavy white card
cutting tool glue pencil
12 transparent containers
paint and paint brush
coloured paper

1 With a compass draw two circles 42 cm in diameter on the card. Cut them out. Inside one disk draw a circle 1·5 cm from the edge. Cut it out. Glue the ring which remains onto the large circle.

2 On the small circle mark 12 divisions. Measure the diameter of the open end of your containers (excluding the lip). Draw this diameter in each of the 12 divisions. Cut them out. Paint the small circle in a bright colour. Leave the large one white.

3 Slide the containers up through the holes in the small circle. Glue them into place.

4 Cut out 12 paper labels. Glue them to the coloured circle by the containers.

7 The wheel is ready for its contents. Place the specimens onto the white circle. Position the coloured circle so that the cups cover the specimens. Write any details about individual specimens onto each card.

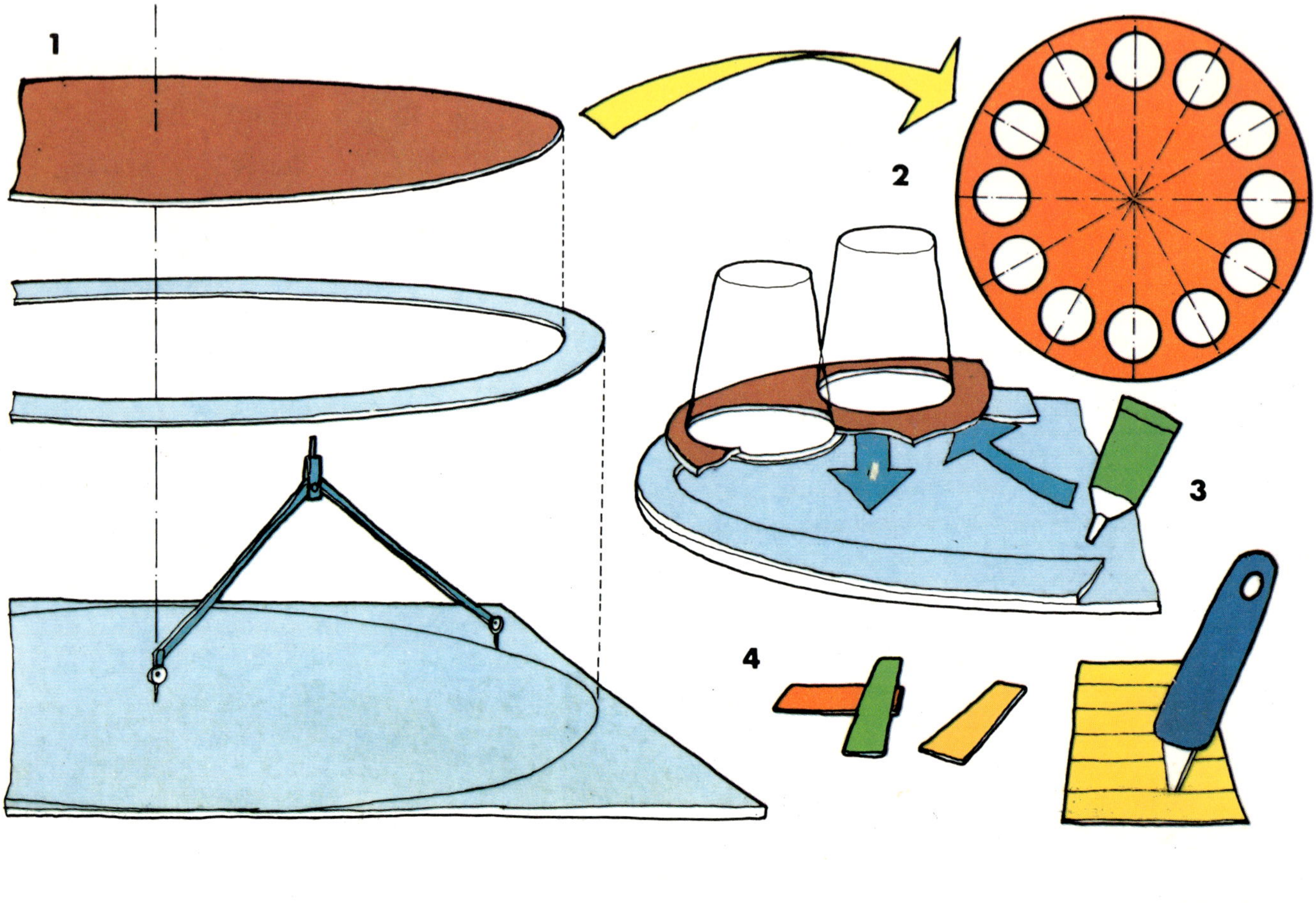

PIN CONES

You will need:

large stopper corks
paint and paint brush
cutting tool
acetate
transparent tape

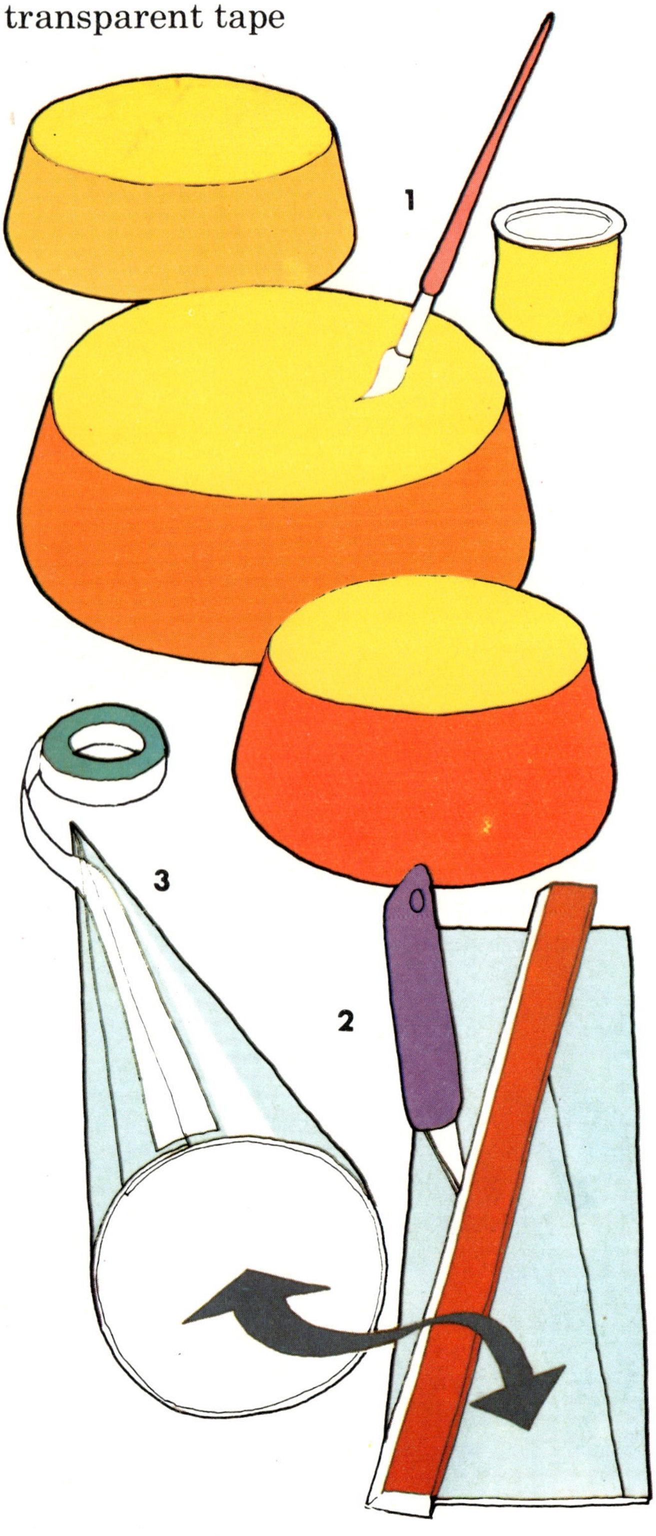

1 Paint the cork. (If you cannot get cork stoppers, cut circles of balsa wood or polystyrene.)

2 Cut out a long triangle of acetate.

3 Using the cork as a base with its larger surface downward, roll the triangle of acetate into a cone. Fix it along the whole length of the join with a strip of transparent sticky tape.

You have now made one pin display unit. Slide the cone off the cork base and push the point of the pin or pins to be displayed into the base. Replace the cone. Make as many pin cones as you have pins.

COIN DISPLAY

You will need:

heavy card
coloured paper
cutting tool
glue 50 rubber bands

1 Cut 9 pieces of card 50 × 6·5 cm and 1 piece 50 × 5·5 cm.

2 Glue yellow paper on one side of the small piece and 5 of the larger pieces. Glue. red paper onto the others.

3 On the coloured side of 3 yellow and 4 red pieces mark and cut sets of V-shaped notches. These are anchor points for the rubber bands.

4 Starting with a red piece, tape all the notched pieces together from the back in alternate colours so they can be folded like a fan.

5 Form a U-shape from the remaining 3 yellow pieces, with the narrow one at the base. Join the sides with tape. Fix one side with a right angled wedge of card so it holds that side upright. Cut a notch at the top centre of each upright. Attach one end of the display slats to the solid upright.
Fix a rubber band on each pair of notches and place coins in them. Close the display and lock it with a rubber band which joins the outside notches. The U-shape now encloses the whole unit.

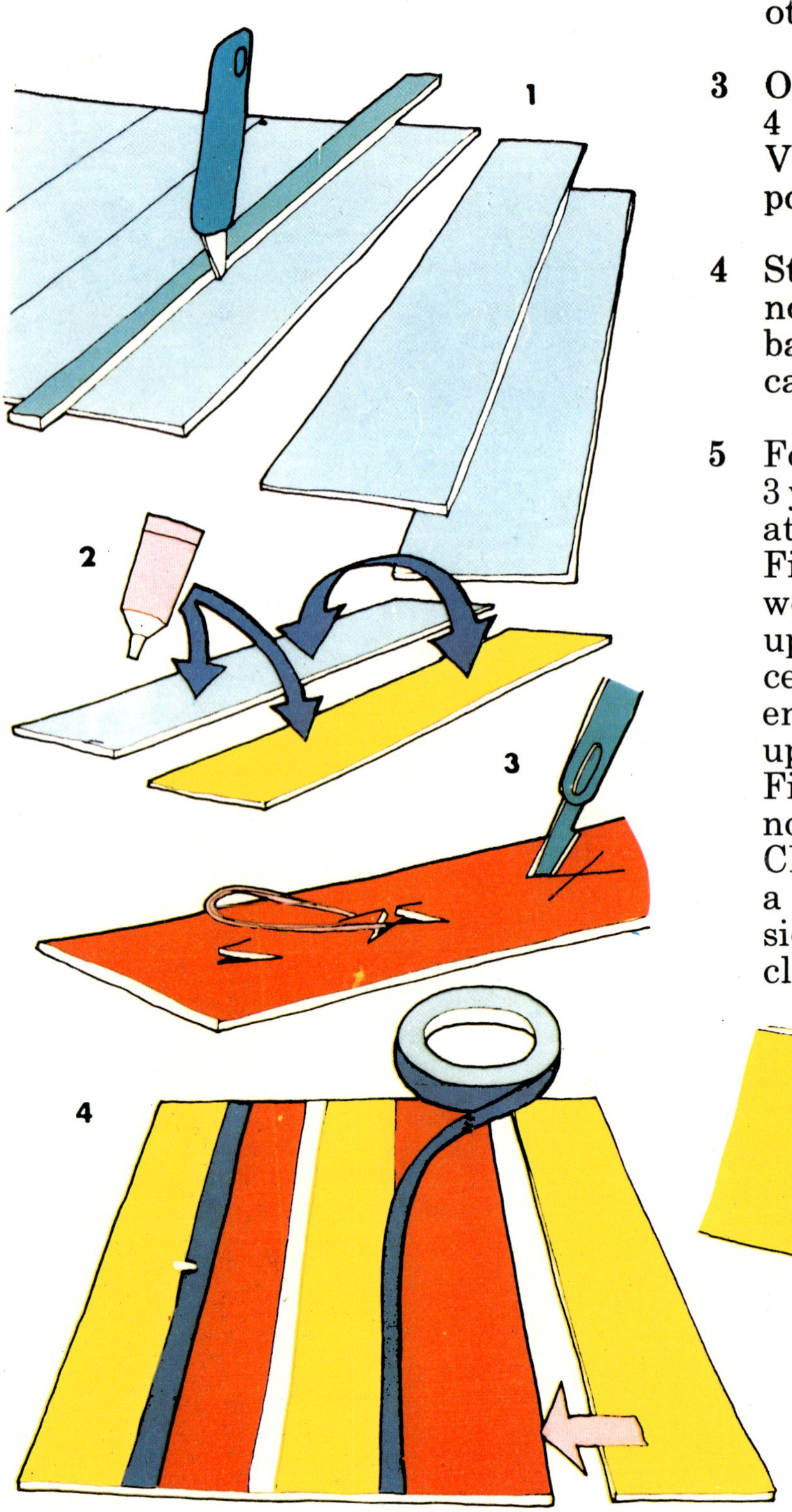

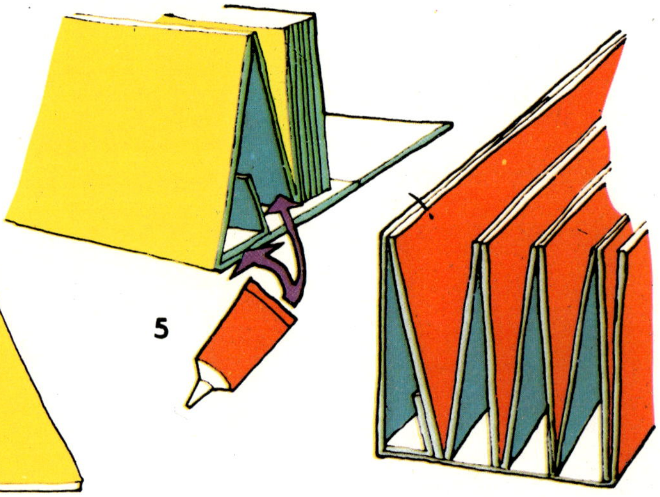

THE GOVERNMENT OF CEYLON
ONE RUPEE
JAPANESE GOVERNMENT
FIVE CENTS

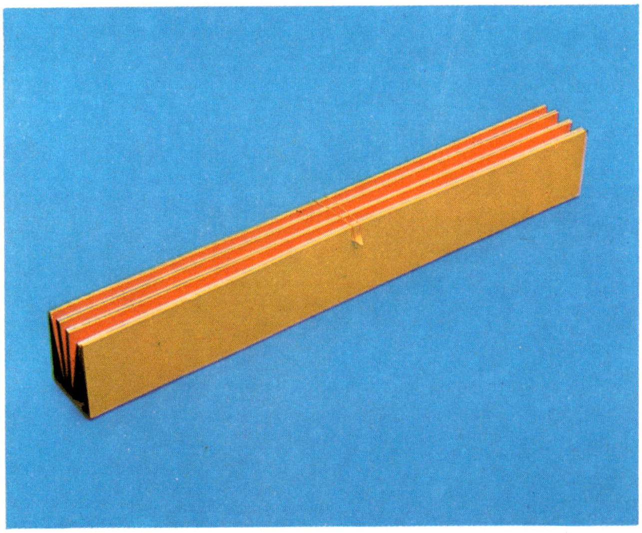

POSTCARD KEEPER

You will need:

coloured card
ruler pencil
cutting tool
glue
paint and paint brush

1 Enlarge the measured diagrams a, b and c onto the card, making one each of a and b, two of c.
Cut out the shapes.
Score along the dotted fold lines.

2 Fold and glue one part c to the base a. Repeat with the other part.

3 Fold and glue part b between the two c parts.

4 Fold the back and front of the base upwards. Glue them in position. Paint the face.

Store your postcard collection in your card keeper. Flick them over both to display them and to change the appearance of the card keeper. Different size cards will alter its hairdo.

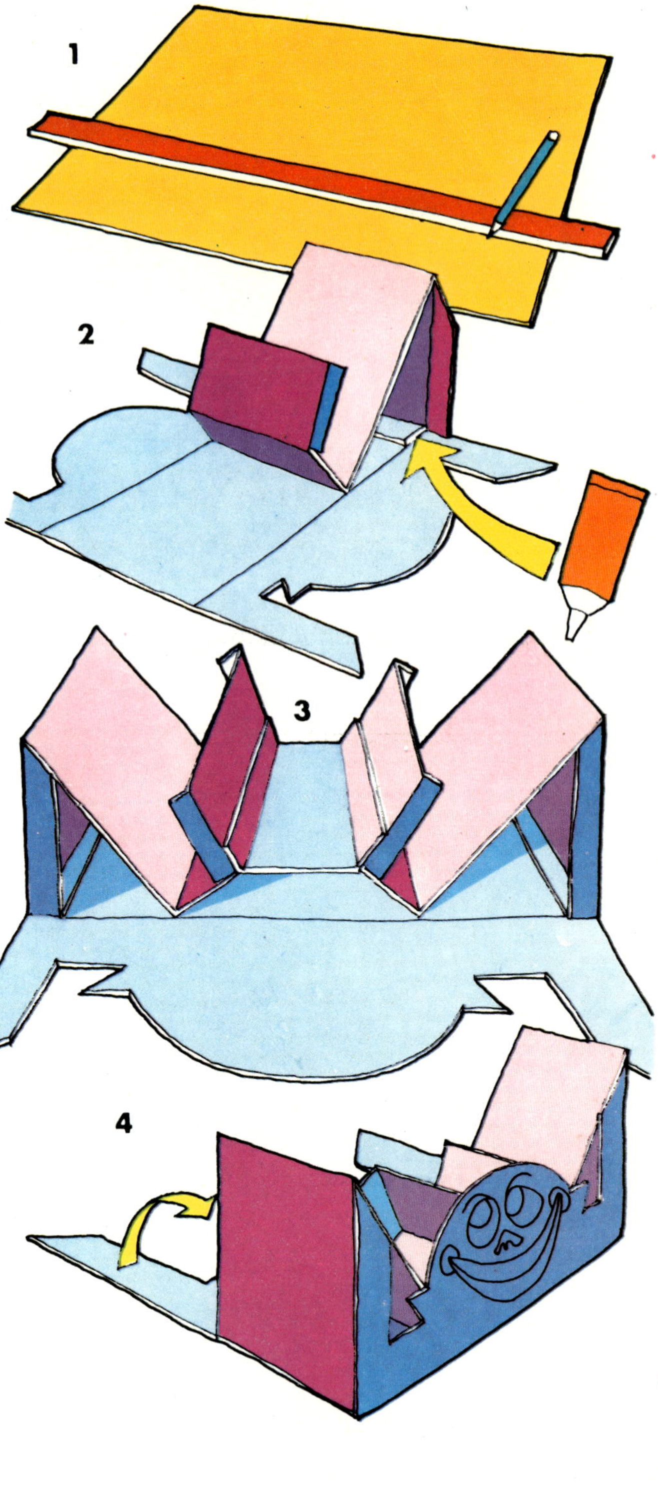

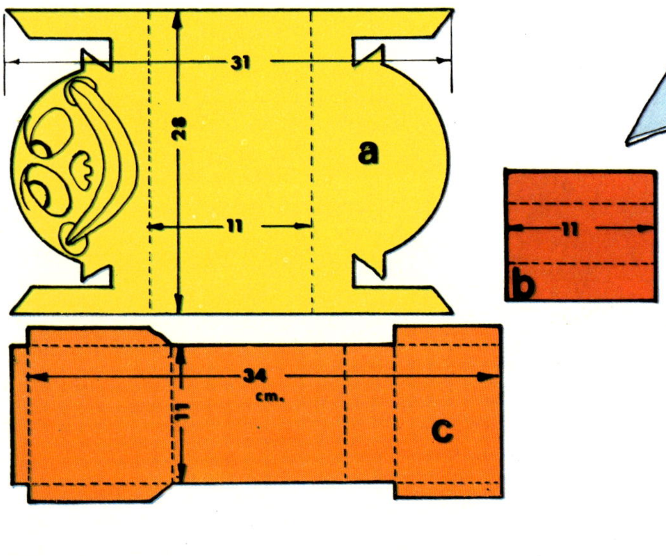

BUTTON TRAYS

You will need:

lengths of wood 1 × 1 cm
saw   cutting tool   drill
5 coloured inks and brush
thick card   2 drawing pins
11 cm dowel rod 55 mm diameter

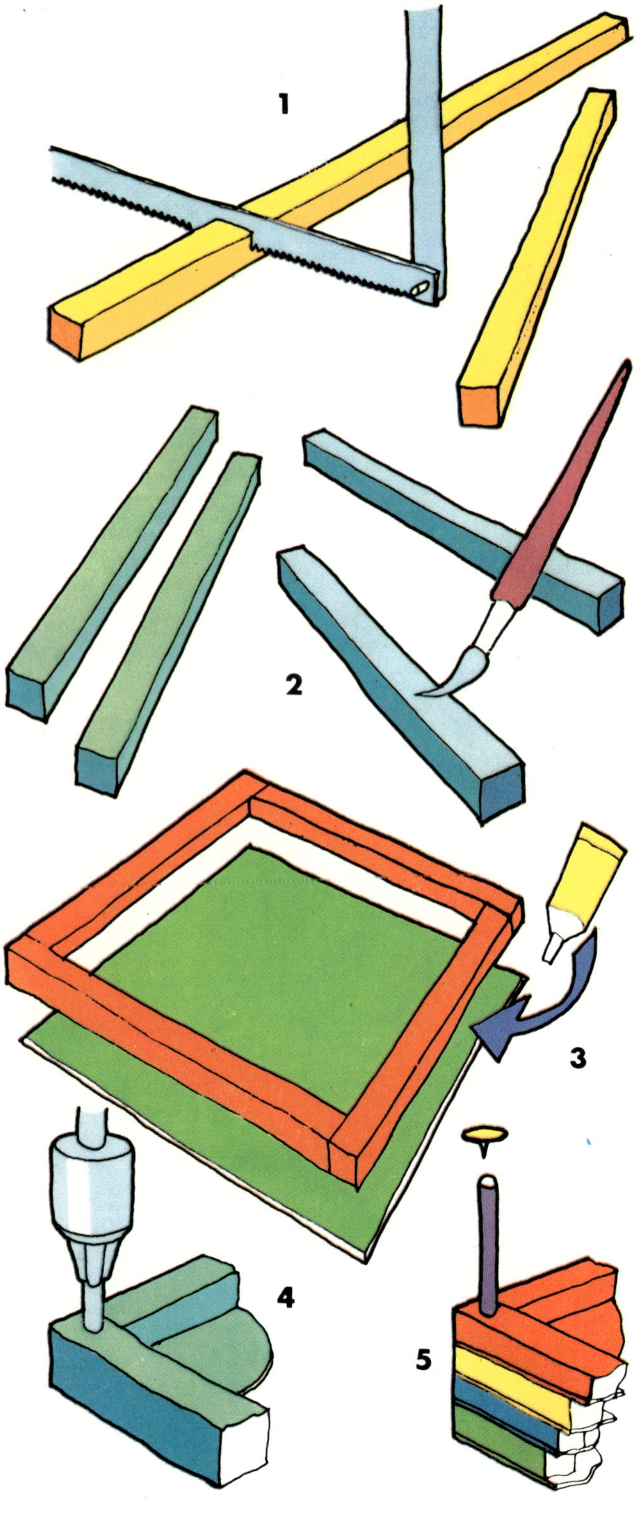

1 Cut 40 14 cm lengths of wood.

2 Paint 8 lengths in each colour.

3 Cut out 11 pieces of card 15 cm square. Paint them. Glue 4 lengths of wood together to make a frame. Make 10 frames and glue them to the card bases to make 10 trays.

4 Drill a hole through one corner of each tray.

5 Put the trays one on top of each other. Pass the dowel rod through them. Add the eleventh piece of card as a lid. Fix a drawing pin in the ends of the dowel rod to hold it in place.

THINGS TO WEAR

HAND JEWELLERY STAND

You will need:

plaster bucket
cardboard
rubber glove
rubber bands
cutting tool
paint and paint brush
block of wood or cork
glue

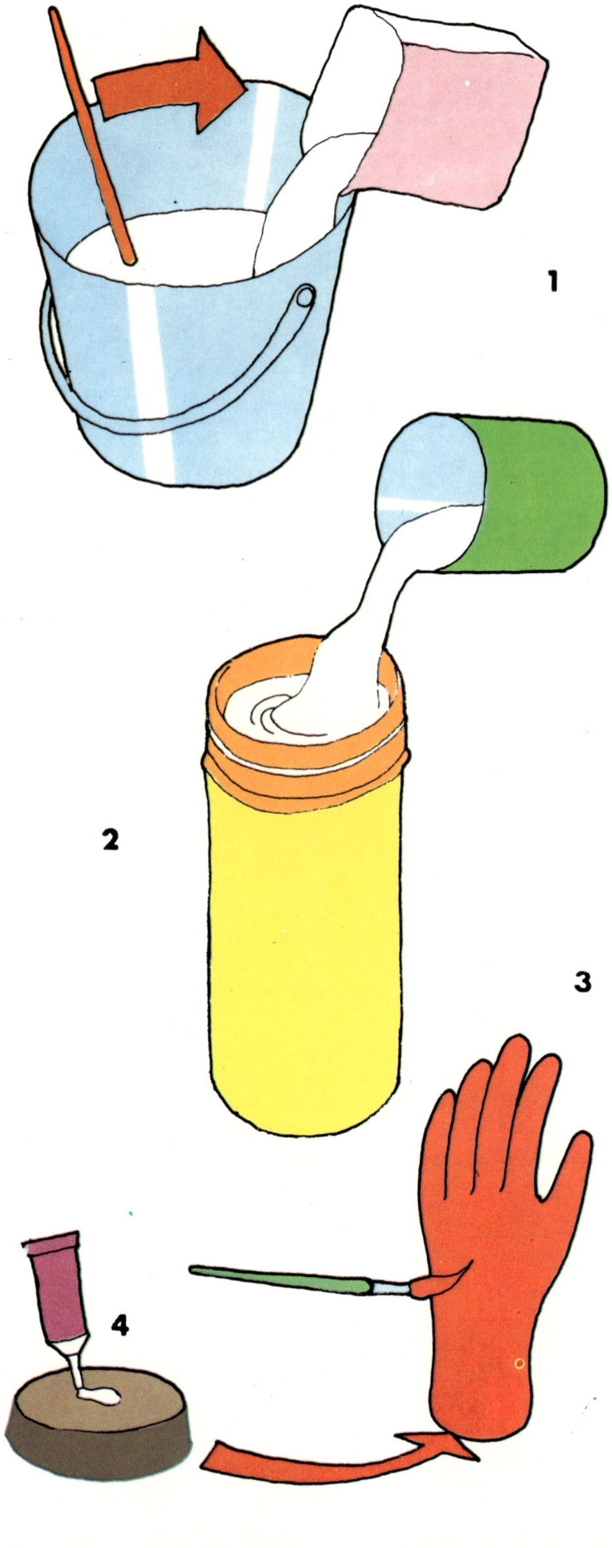

1 Mix the plaster in a bucket so that it is like syrup.

2 Roll the cardboard into a cylinder shaped wide enough to fit the rubber glove plus a little extra to allow for expansion. Secure with a rubber band.
Push the rubber glove down into the cylinder bringing the wrist of the glove up over the edge. Secure it with a rubber band.
Ask a friend to hold the cylinder in a place where it won't matter if any plaster is spilt. (DON'T hold it over a sink or the sink will block!)
Carefully pour the plaster into the glove.
Allow the plaster to dry inside the cylinder.
The cylinder should stand firmly on its own. This will take approximately one hour.

3 When the plaster is dry release the rubber band, unroll the cardboard and cut away the rubber glove from the plaster.
Paint the hand all over in one colour of your own choice.

4 Glue the hand to the block of wood to make a stand. Hang your jewellery onto your hand stand.

TUBE BRACELET

You will need:

clear plastic tubing
scissors
dowel
ink or oil

You can buy plastic tubing at a hardware or aquarium store. Cut it to the length you require.
To join the lengths use one of these methods.

1 Expand the opening at one end of the tube with the ends of the scissors. Force the other end in tightly.

2 Push a small length of dowel into one end of the tube, then link it to the other end.

3 There are various ways to decorate the tubes. Nearly fill the tubes with a coloured liquid like ink or coloured ink plus oil to make a two-colour combination which can move in the tube. If you use this method the link must be water-tight. Nearly fill the tubes with coloured beads. Pack the tubes with coloured thread.

1

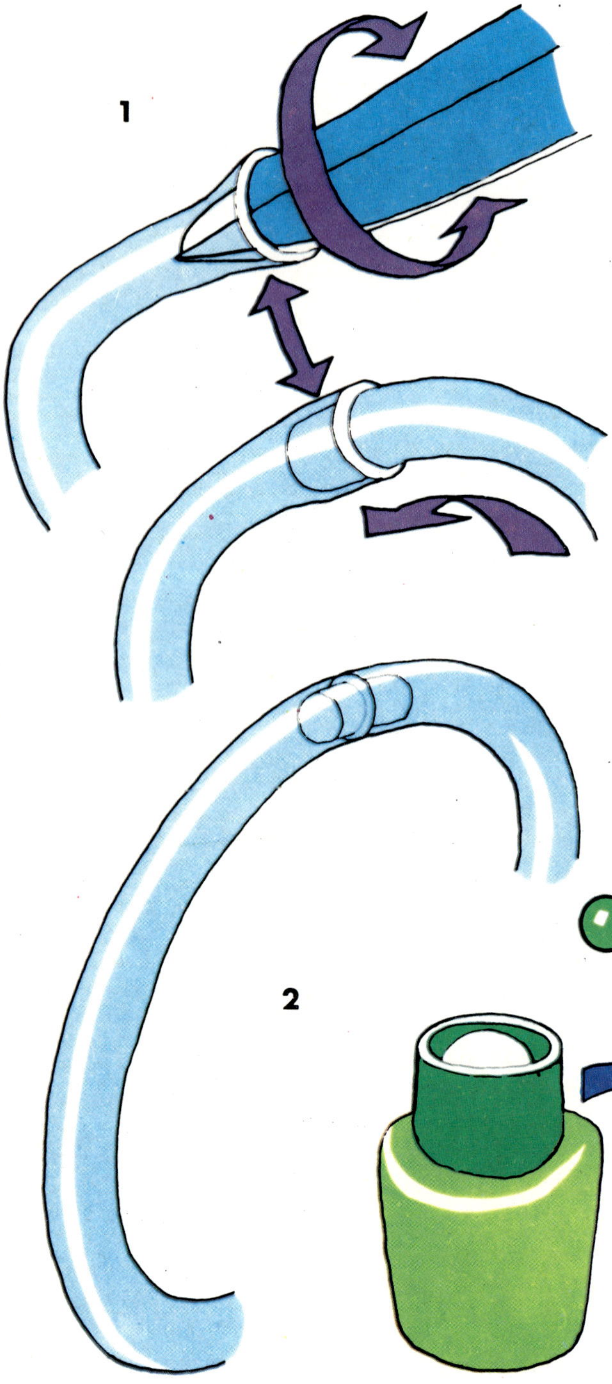

2

3

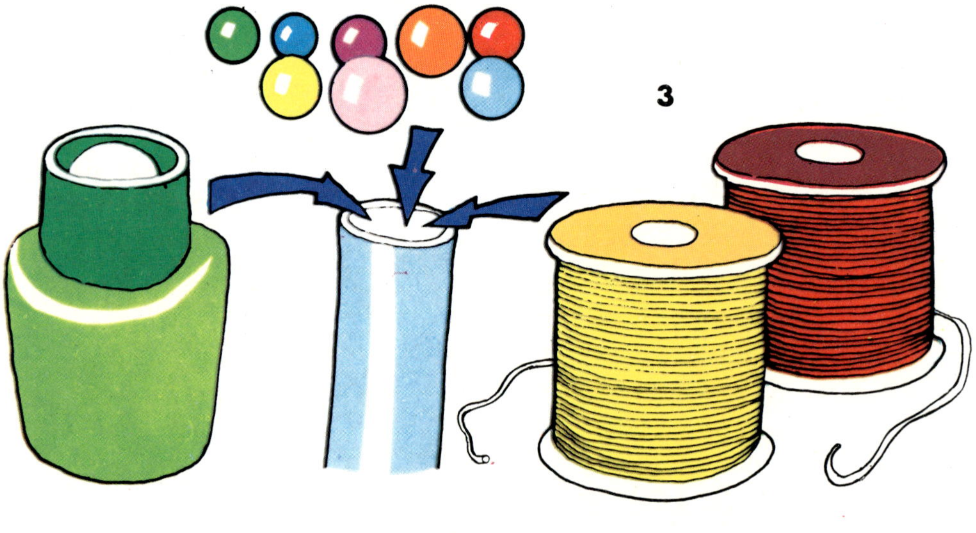

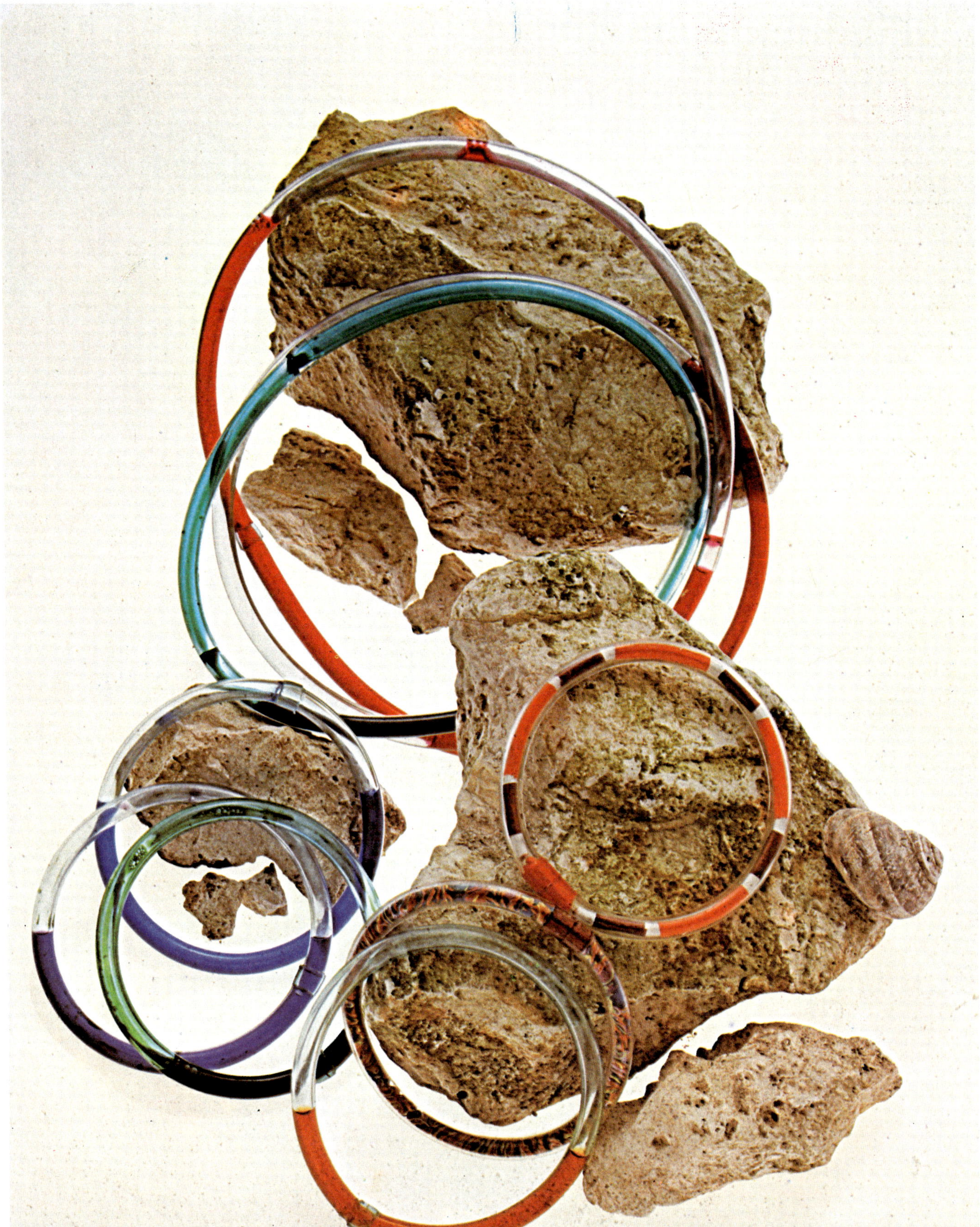

KEY RINGS

You will need:

thin plywood   veneer
fretsaw   vice   file
paint and paint brush
cutting tool   glue   drill
nylon twine   pliers   key ring

1 Using the fretsaw, cut out the shape you have chosen from the plywood.

2 Finish off the edges carefully with a fine file.

3 Paint your design on to the key fob.

4 An alternative method of decoration is to cut the design from veneer and glue it on to the fob. You can then paint the veneer and the background. We show here the signs of the zodiac which you can use in this way.

5 Drill a hole in the edge of the fob. Tie a twist of nylon twine through this hole for your keys. You can either tie your keys directly on to the twine or use a key ring. For the elephant fob use a wire spring for the trunk, clipping it on to the wood firmly with pliers.

RINGS

You will need:

ring mounts
plastic tube scissors glue
acetate or celluloid balsa tape
2 wooden beads
wire paint
rice feather toothpick

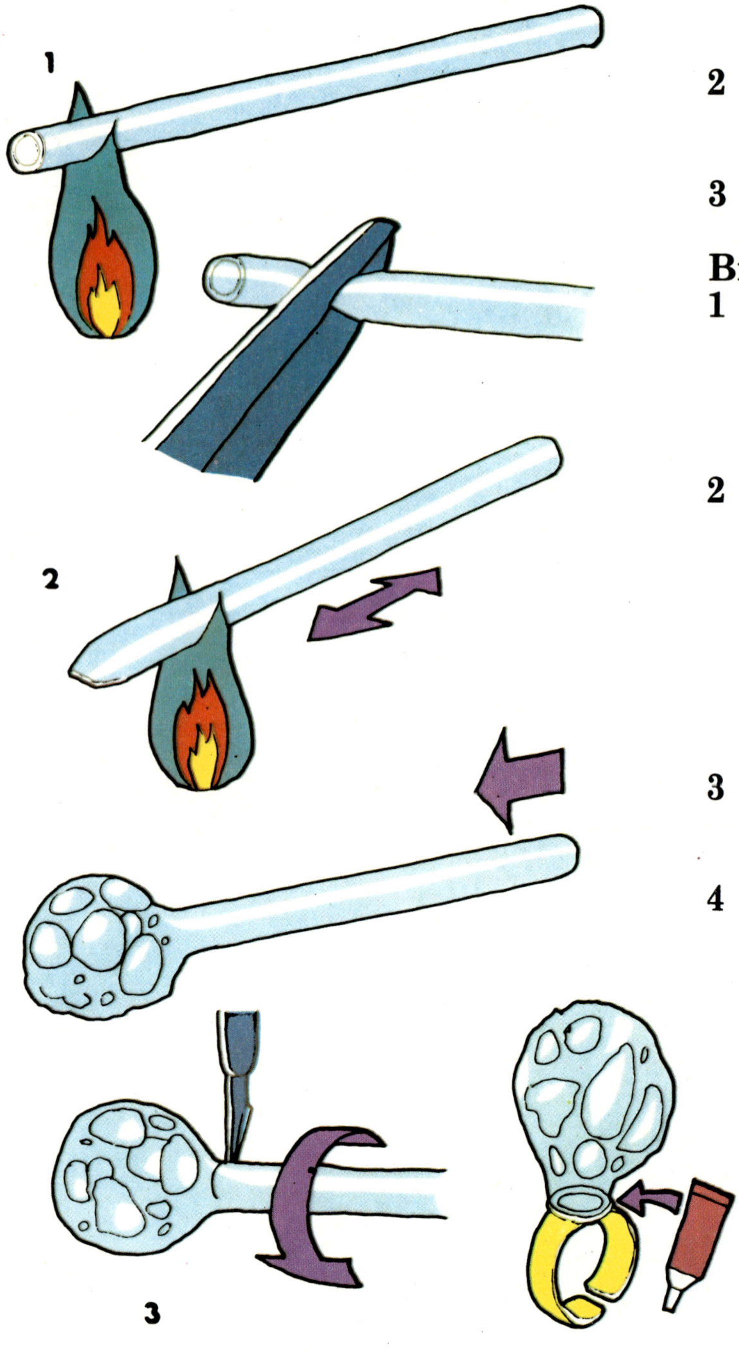

Plastic Ring

1 Heat one end of the plastic tube and cut it off to seal the tube.

2 Heat the end again. Blow into the other end so that the tube inflates.

3 Cut off bulb. Glue to mount.

Bird Ring and Rice Ring

1 Cut out 5 pieces of acetate each 2 cm square. Stick them together with tape. Cut a piece of balsa the same size to use as a base.

2 Stick the beads together to form the bird's head and body. Stick a piece of a toothpick to the head for a beak and a feather to the body for a tail. Slip a piece of wire into the bigger bead so the bird can be attached to the base.

3 The other ring can be filled with rice dyed in different colours.

4 Insert base and glue rings to mount.

2

3

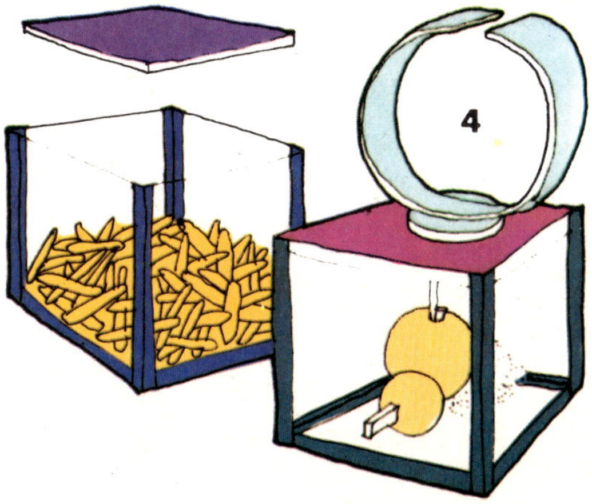

4

FUN GLASSES

You will need:

acetate or celluloid
card
cutting tool
glue
paint and brush

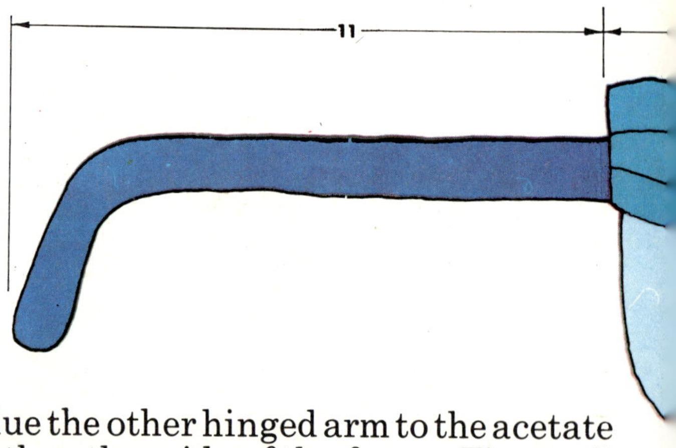

Seaside Glasses
Cut the mount of the glasses from the card all in one piece including the yacht and arms as shown in the diagram above. Paint the yacht and the sea.

Cut a piece of light blue acetate to the shape and size shown in the diagram, 13 cm wide and 8 cm high. Tape the acetate to the back of the mount.

Cut another piece of light card the shape of the mount without the arms. Glue it to the mount over the back of the acetate.

At the front of the first mount, where the sea area meets the arms, make a vertical score so that the arms can be bent backward.

Moon and Star Glasses
Cut the following pieces of card to the shape and dimensions shown in the diagram: 2 arms in purple card, allowing an extra 5 mm for the hinge; 2 yellow frames; 1 pink star. Cut out the centres of the frames very carefully. Cut a piece of yellow or orange acetate the size of the outside measurements of the yellow frames. Glue the acetate between the two yellow frames.

Glue the pink star in position on the front of the frame.

Glue one hinged arm to the acetate behind the star.

Glue the other hinged arm to the acetate at the other side of the frame. Fix small strips of card to the front of the glasses to conceal this hinge.

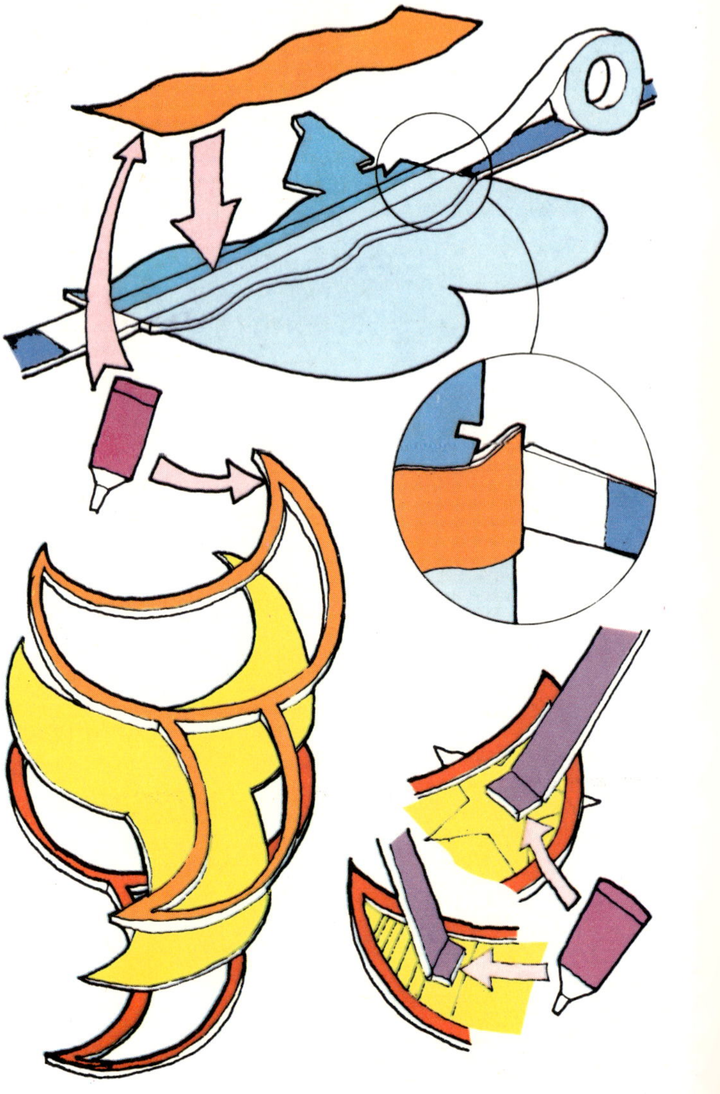

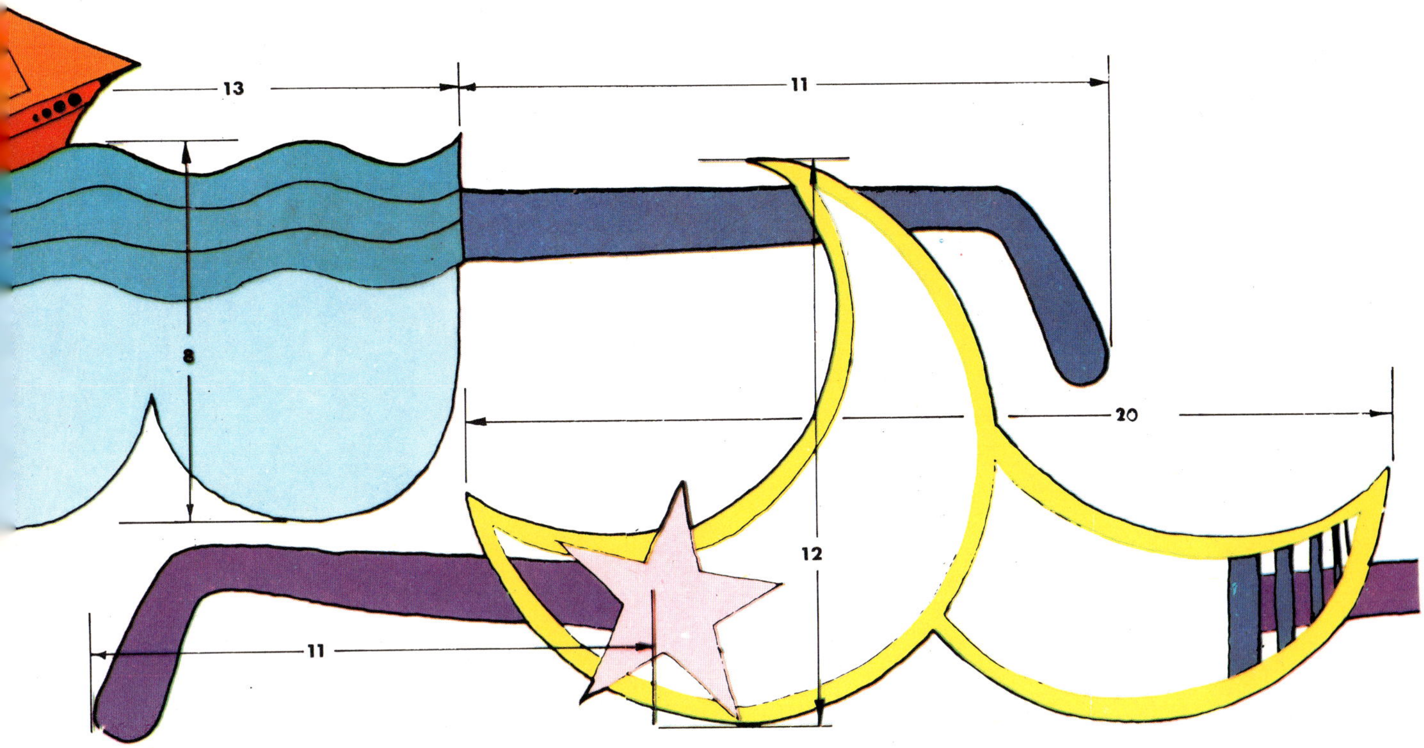
13
11
8
20
12
11

PURSE BELT

You will need:

thin plywood canvas
fretsaw file cutting tool
paint and paint brush
glue punch vice
string wool

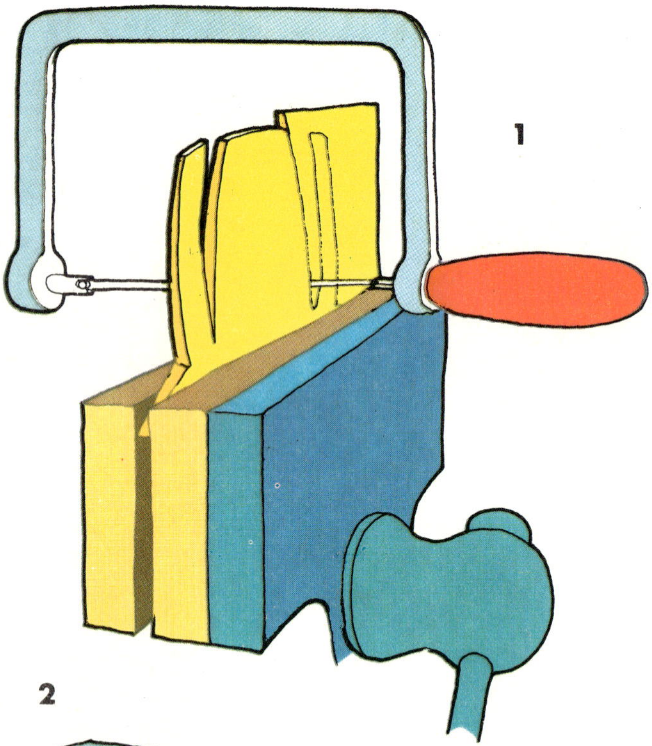

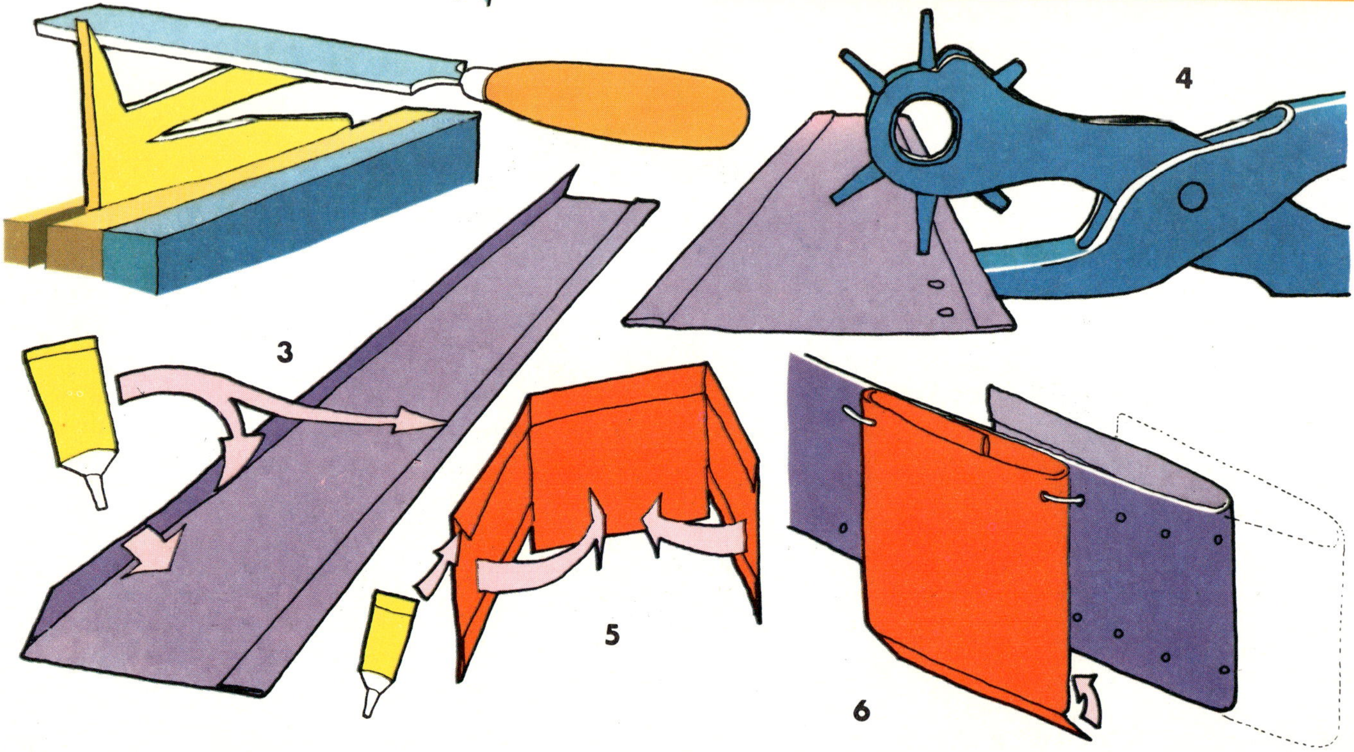

1 Using the fretsaw, cut out the shape of the buckle making it about 5–6 cm deep.

2 Smooth and shape the buckle with the file. Paint the bull's features on to the buckle.

3 Cut a strip of canvas about 7 cm deep and 16 cm longer than the required waist length. Fold over the two long edges and glue them down firmly.

4 Punch holes 2 cm apart along both edges of the belt.

5 Make 2 pockets from contrasting canvas, folding and gluing them into shape as shown. The pockets can be as long and as wide as you need. Punch holes in the *back* of each pocket 2 cm apart to match the holes in the belt.

6 Attach the pockets to the belt with string. Use the string to fold down the ends of the belt to form holders for the buckle to be slipped into.

Finish off by binding the edges with wool.

PAPER BELT

You will need:

heavy card
cutting tool
coloured magazine paper
glue
needle
elastic thread

1 From the heavy card cut a triangle of the dimensions shown. Use this as a pattern to cut out triangles of coloured magazine paper. You will need about 70 triangles, depending on the size of your waist.

2 Roll the triangles from the wide end into tight rolls.

3 Put glue on the end to fix them.

4 Join all the pieces with the elastic thread. First sew through the top of the pieces, then through the bottom. When you return the thread for the bottom row, leave a loop of elastic for the fastening.

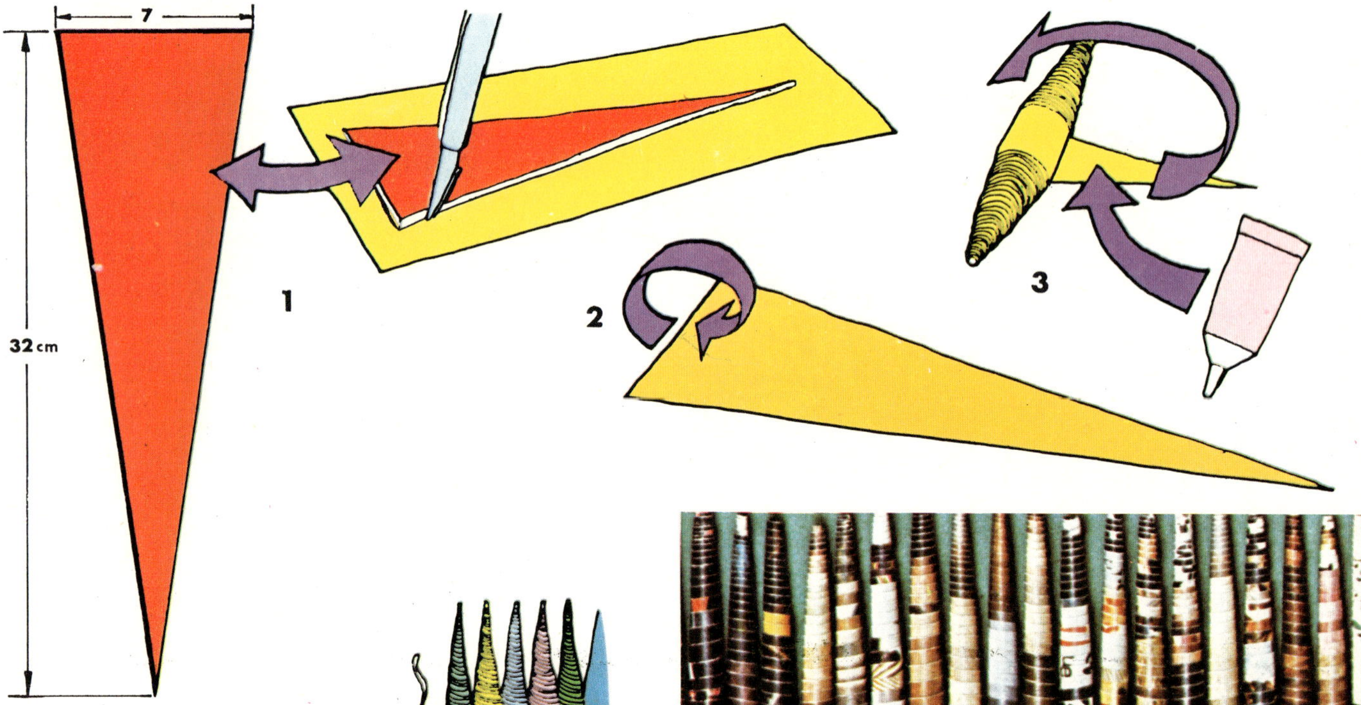

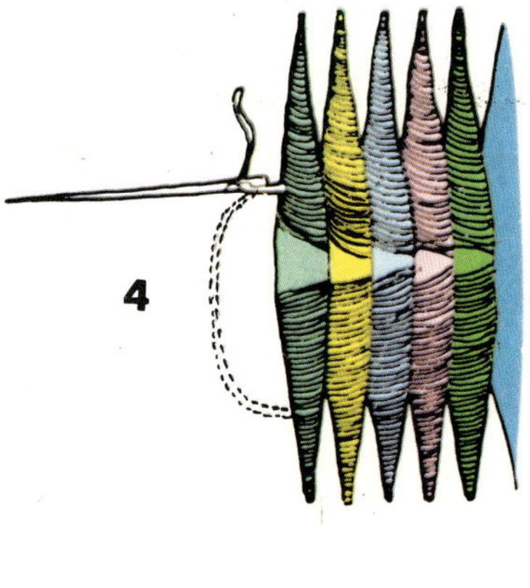

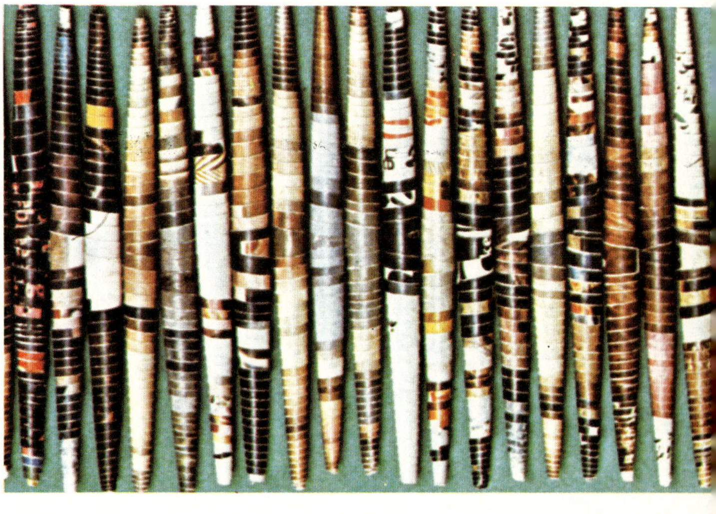

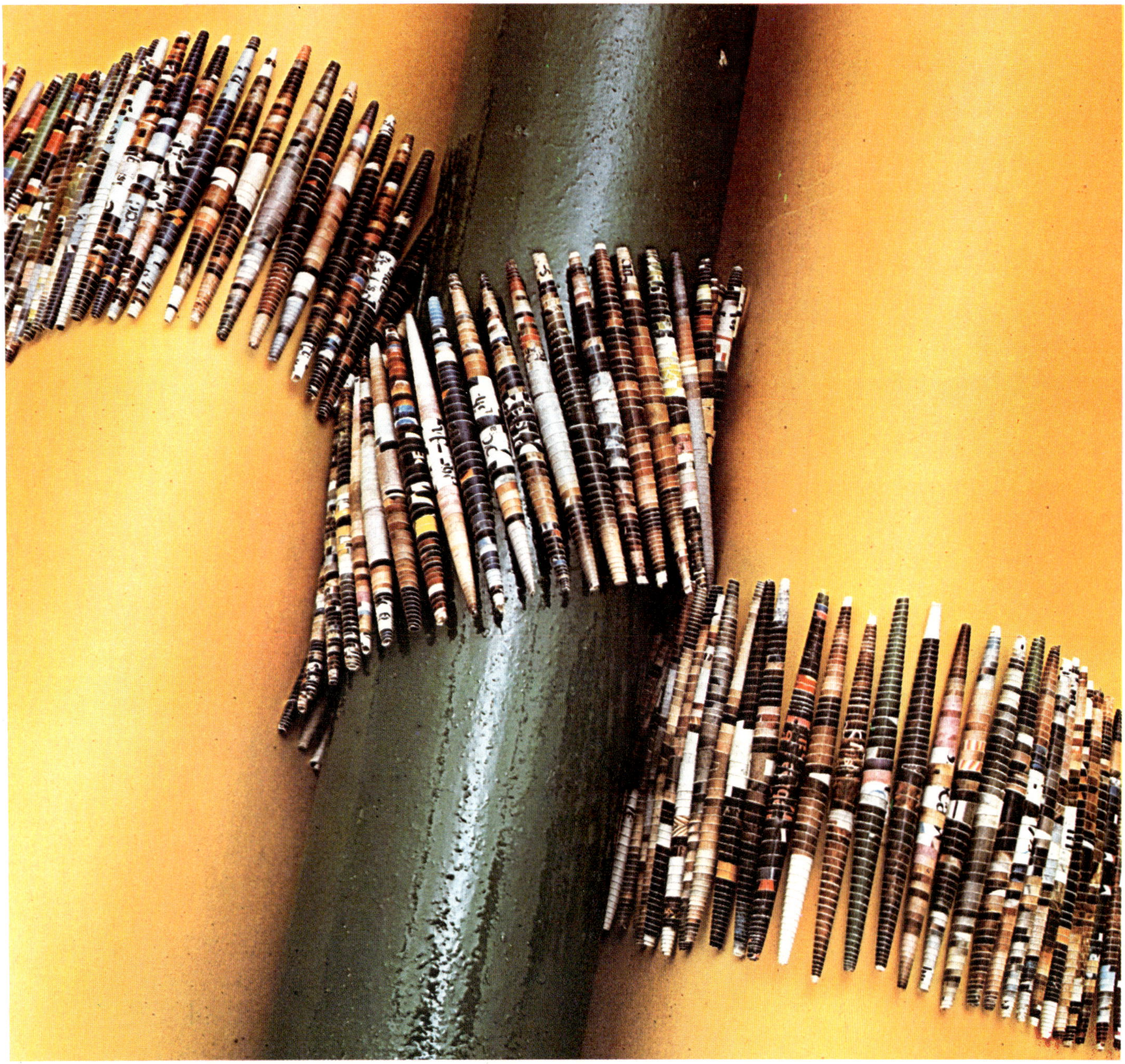

PENCIL BUCKLE

You will need:

7 coloured pencils
cutting tool   stapler
card   glue
wide elastic   clasp
needle   strong thread

1 Cut two lengths of each size shown from the 7 different coloured pencils. Cut two triangles of heavy card as shown in the diagram.

2 You will need some wide elastic a bit smaller than the size of your waist. On the back of the elastic sew a clasp to join the belt.

3 On the other side of the elastic staple the card triangles to form the buckle.

4 Now glue the lengths of pencil to the two card triangles in descending order of size to form the buckle of your belt. You will need strong glue and you should let it dry thoroughly.

2

1

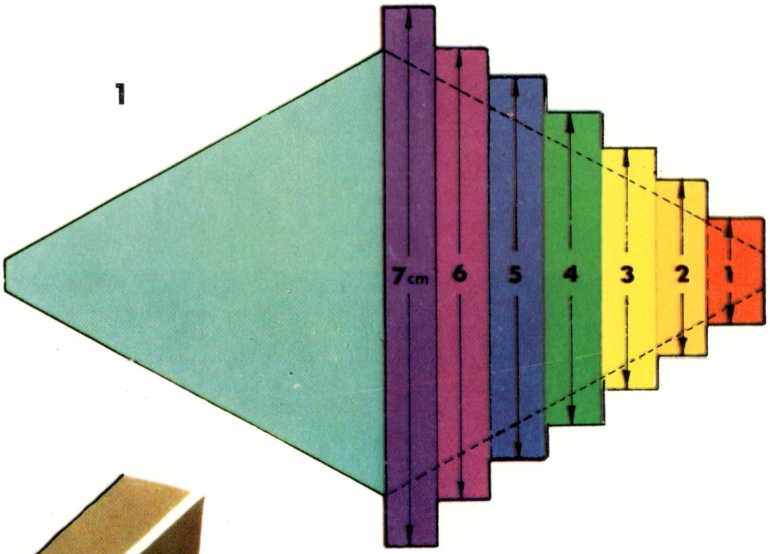

3

4

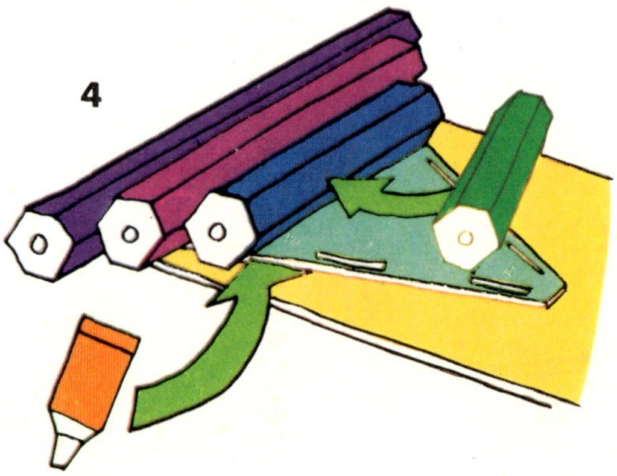

APPLETREE APRON

You will need:

yellow, red, brown and green cloth
soft cord
paper and pencil
needle and thread
scissors   pins

Make enlargements of pieces b, c and d on the paper to make your pattern.

Cut out a piece of yellow material approximately 65 × 85 cm for the apron. Hem it all the way round, leaving a wider open-ended hem for the draw cord at the top.

Cut out the tree shape 'c' and the grass shape 'd' in green, the 2 trunk shapes 'b' in brown and the apples in red.

Sew the apples onto the tree shape, leaving the top open as pockets. Sew one piece of trunk to the other so that it makes another pocket. Sew the apple tree and grass down onto the apron.

Attach waist and neck ties.

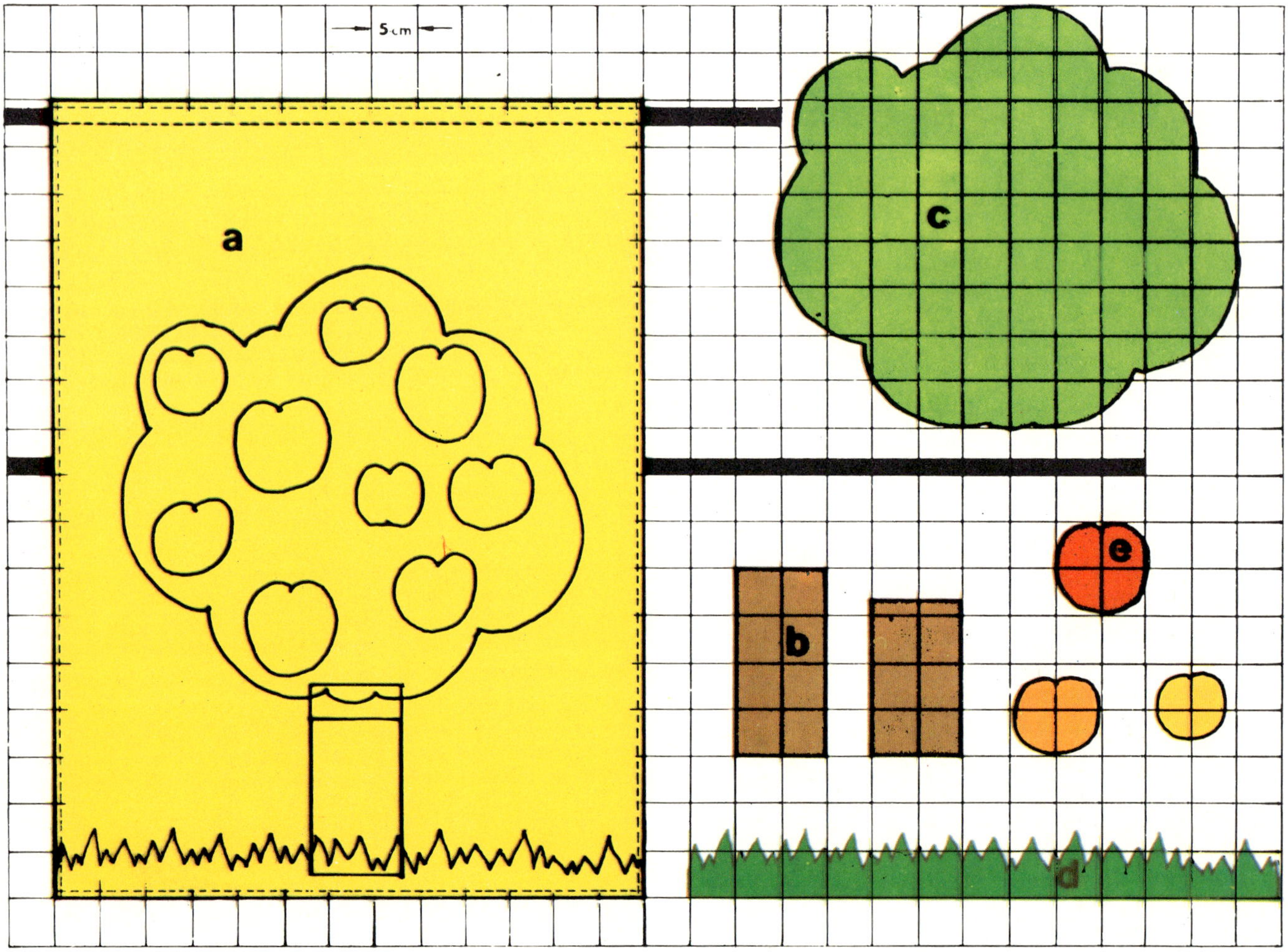

DECORATING YOUR ROOM

BRIGHTEN UP YOUR FURNITURE

You will need:

sandpaper
white undercoat paint
bright enamel paints
paint brushes
pencil

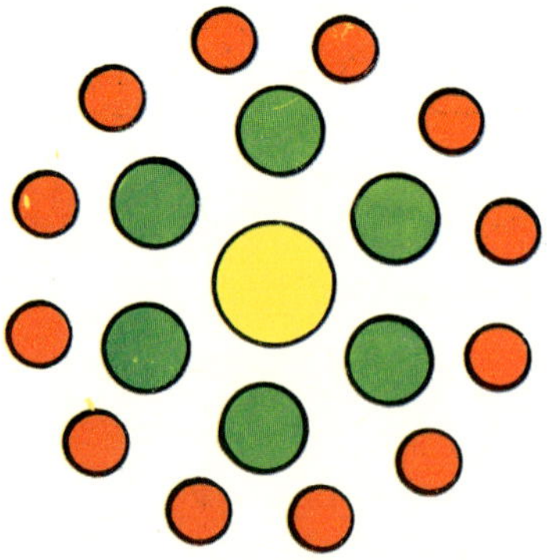

The drawing shows:
a a picture frame **c** a tray
b a chair **d** a mirror

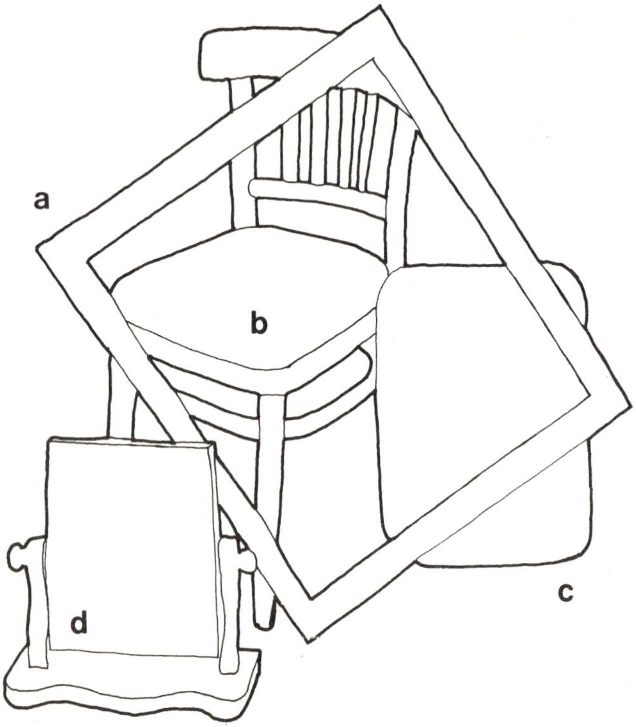

1 Clean all the surfaces of the article you are going to paint with sandpaper to remove old paint and grease. Paint the surfaces with the white undercoat. Allow it to dry thoroughly.

2 Draw your chosen design onto the dry undercoat.

3 Paint in the design, painting the background first.

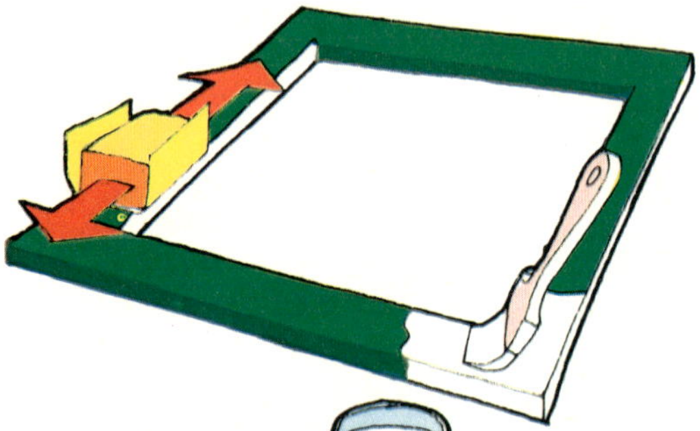
1

2

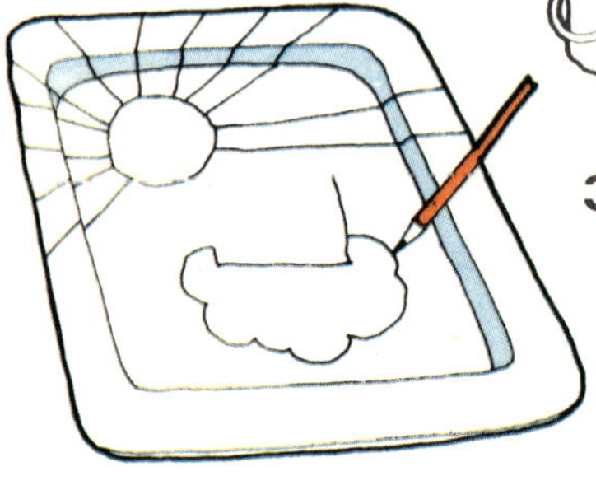
3

4

WINDOW STAR

You will need:

large sheet of stiff card
pencil or pen   ruler
cutting tool
dark paint and paint brush
sheets of cellophane

This star gives the effect of a stained glass window.
The material suggested is cellophane, but the effect will be even better if you use acetate or cinemoid.

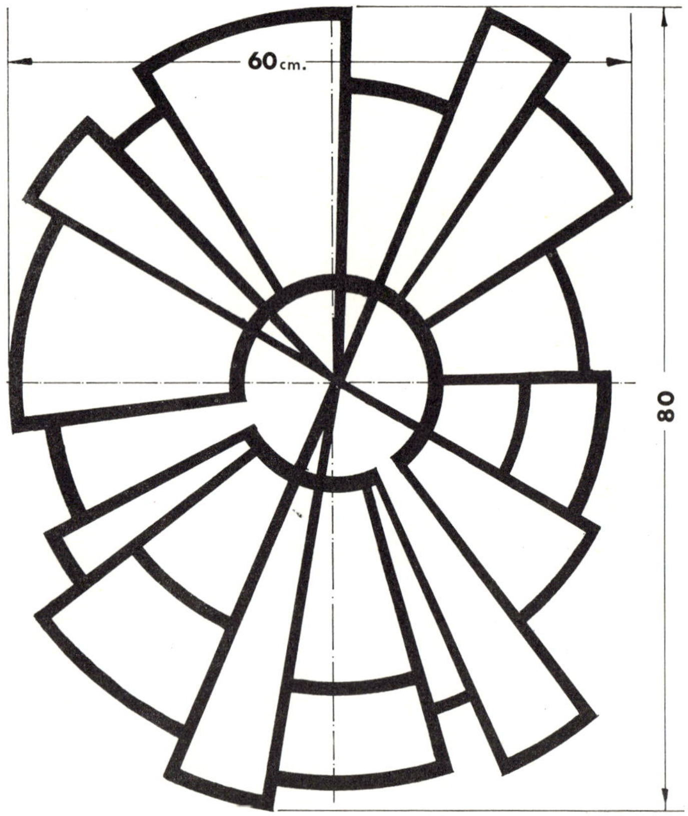

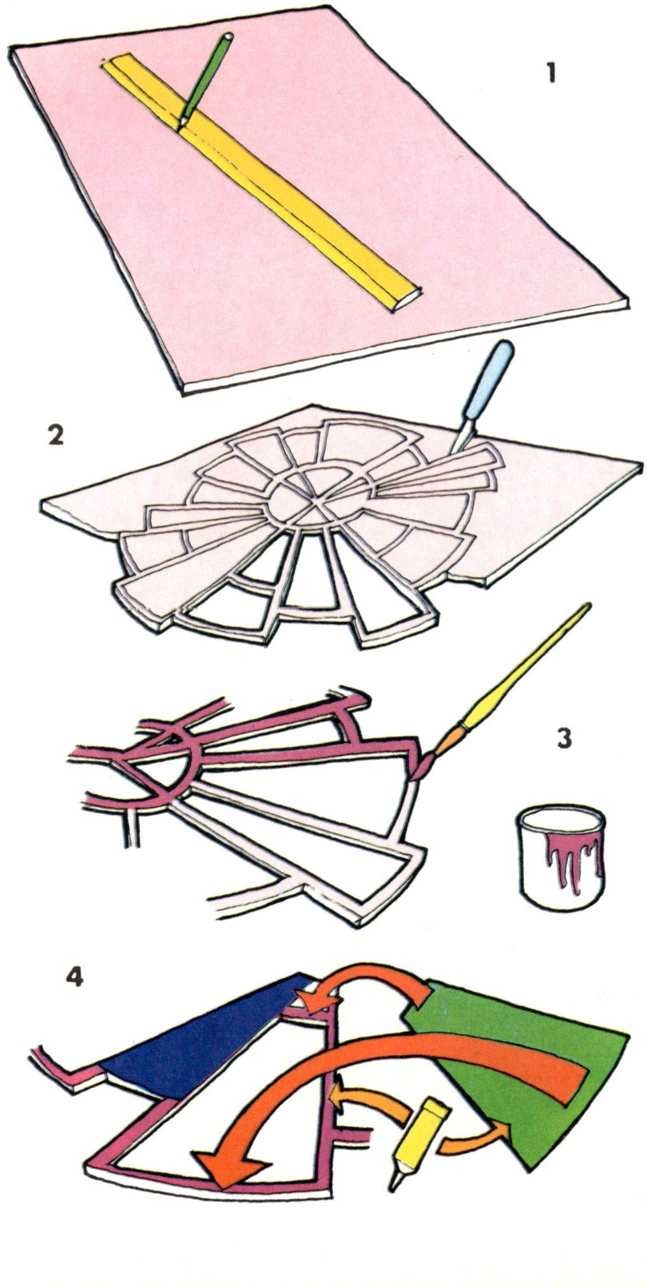

1 Enlarge the design onto the card. The width of the dividing lines should be about 1·5 cm.

2 Cut out the frame from the card.

3 Paint the frame a dark colour.

4 Cut out shapes from the cellophane or other material to fit over the openings in the frame.
Glue these shapes carefully onto the back of the frame.

STRAW CURTAIN

You will need:

drinking straws
coloured beads or buttons
paint and paint brush (optional)
wool
drawing pins

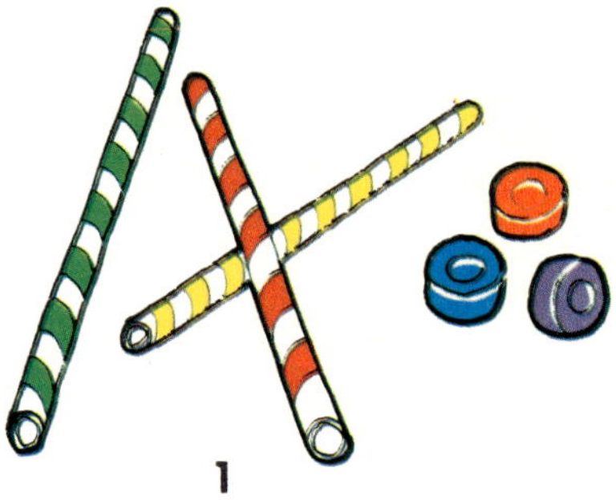

1

2

3

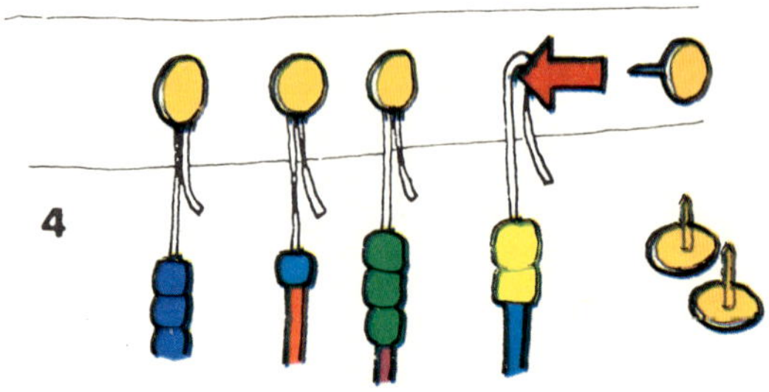

4

You can use a straw curtain like this over a door or window or as a room divider. The curtain can be as big or as small as you feel like making it.

1 You can paint the straws if you want to do so.

2 Cut lengths of wool longer than the window to be covered.
Pin one end of a length of wool in a convenient place.
Begin threading the straws and beads onto the wool. You can thread them either in a regular pattern or at random. The diagram on the left shows one example of how you can build up a pattern.

3 Carefully tie a knot in the last bead to keep the beads and straws in place.

4 Repeat 2 and 3 for all the lengths of wool. Hang each length over your door or window with drawing pins. You can hang each length from a slat of wood and then fix the whole curtain to the door or window frame.

PAPER BLIND

You will need:

coloured light paper   lengths of cord
pencil   ruler   glue
small nails or large pins
cutting tool   2 screws
2 slats of wood, 10 cm wider than paper

1 Score lines across paper 5 cm apart. Fold on these lines like a concertina.

2 Glue the end fold of each sheet and stick the sheets together.

3 Close all the folds together into a block. Drive a nail or large pin through this block about 3 mm from each end. This acts as a marker.

4 Unfold the blind. Cut a 1 cm square round each mark for the cord.

5 Using coins or other shapes as a pattern, cut holes in the blind.

6 Drill one hole at each end of the 2 slats of wood to match the cord holes in the blind. On one slat (A) drill 2 holes side by side 3 cm from the cord hole at one end of the slat. Drill a hole at each end of the slat about 3 cm from the end for fixing the blind to the window frame.

7 Glue the slats of wood to the top and bottom of the blind (slat A on the top). Take care to match up the cord holes on the blind.

8 Pass 2 lengths of cord up through the bottom slat, through the blind and out of the top slat. Fix the cords at the bottom with a small piece of wood or a nail, to stop them slipping through. Pass the cords down the 2 holes at the end of the top slat.

9 Screw the top slat to the top of your window frame.

Choose paper to fit the width of your window and long enough so, when the sheets are stuck together, they will be 15 cm longer than the window's depth.

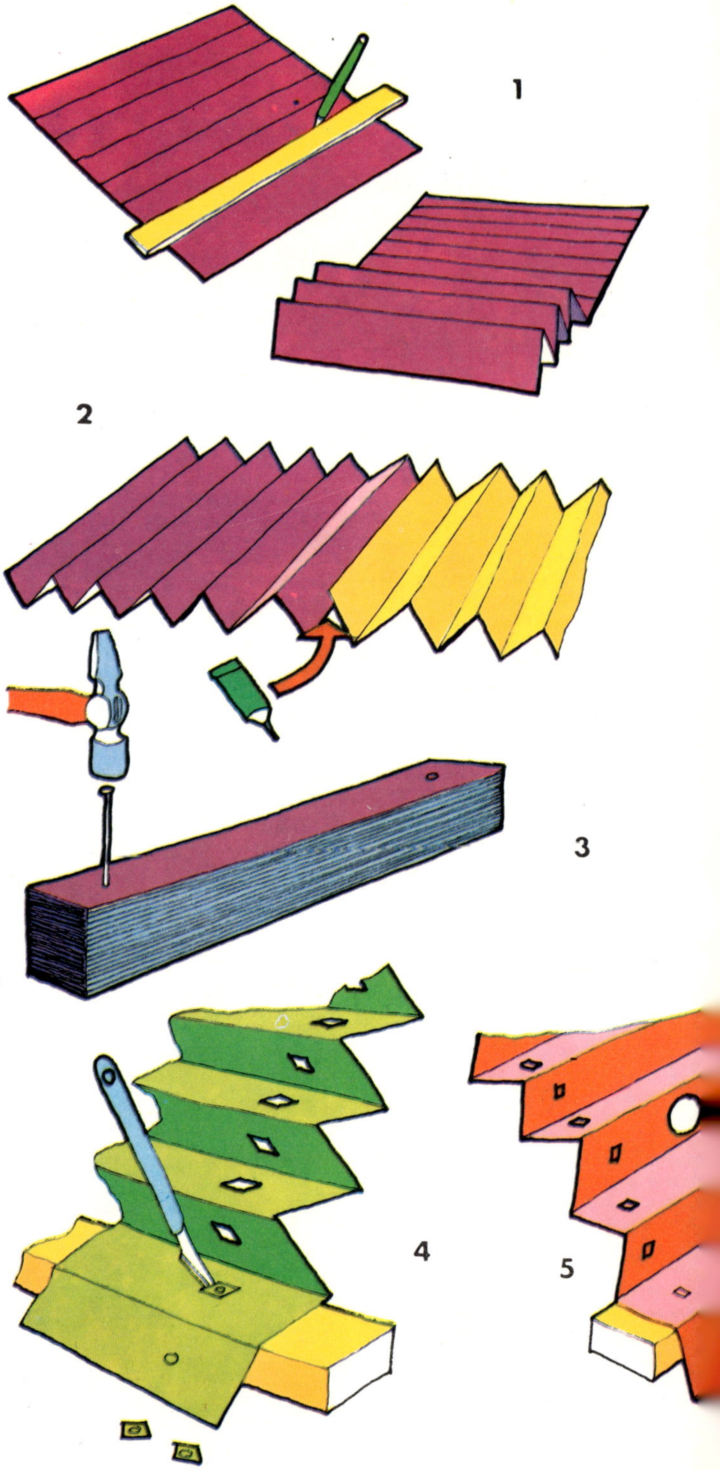

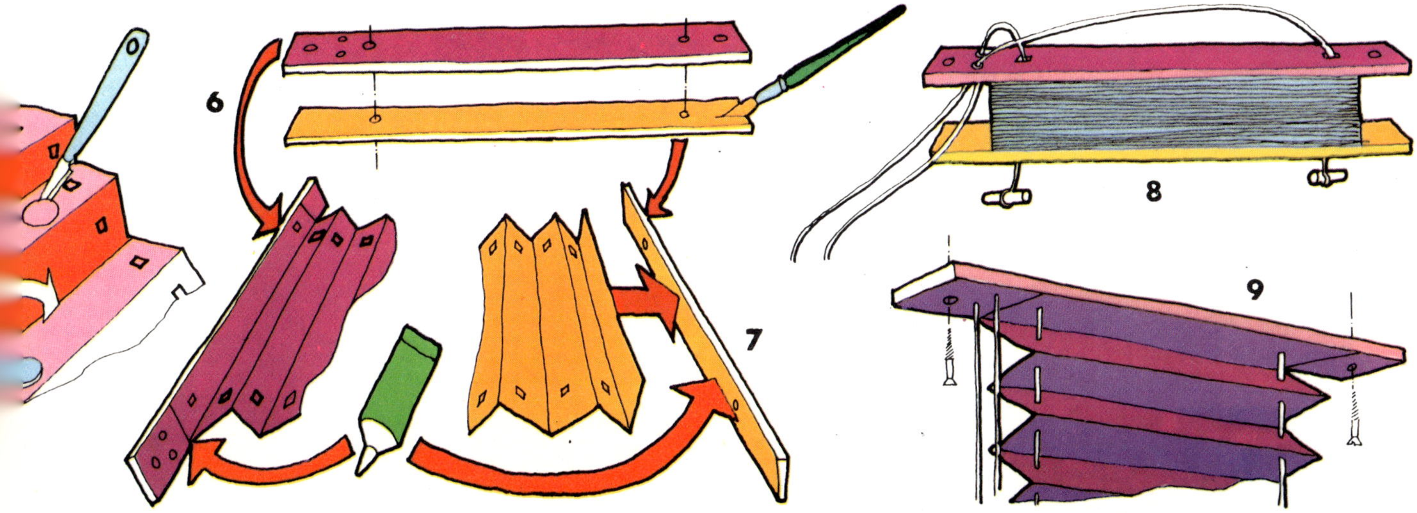
6
7
8
9

WALL FRIEZE

You will need:

card and drawing paper
cutting tool   pencil
paints and paint brush
double sided tape
glue or drawing pins

We show you here how to make a wall frieze of a dragon, but you could create your own using the method described here. You might like a forest or farm scene or a street of houses or a harbour. Perhaps you could make a frieze to go right round your room or to climb the stairs of your house.

1 Using this diagram, draw outline enlargements for each of the nine parts of the frieze. Use the largest card you can manage.

2 Cut out the shapes.

3 Paint each piece.

4 Build up the picture on your wall using the tape, glue or pins. Fix the background first and the dragon itself last.

1
2
3
4

PATCHWORK WALLPAPER

You will need:

a wallpaper sample book
set square
scissors
wallpaper glue   sponge
wallpaper brush
piece of stiff card

This is a way of papering a wall which you have probably never seen before. For a beginner it is certainly much easier than using full rolls of wallpaper. Decorator's shops often have old wallpaper sample books which they are willing to give away when the new designs come into stock.

Cut as many sheets as you will need from the book. Be sure to cut straight and to keep the corners square with the aid of the set square.

1 Put a cloth or newspaper down on the floor to protect it while you work. Wash the wall you are going to paper.

2 Prepare the wallpaper glue according to the instructions on the packet.

3 Lay out all your sheets of wallpaper on the floor in the order in which you want them to appear on the wall you are papering.
Put wallpaper glue on the wall. Then put glue on the back of each sheet of wallpaper as you are ready to put it up.

4 Stick the sheets of wallpaper onto the wall. Press them down with the edge of the piece of stiff card. Wipe off any surplus glue with the damp sponge.

1

WALL DECORATION

You will need:

coloured sticky tapes
pencil
paper
long ruler
piece of stiff card

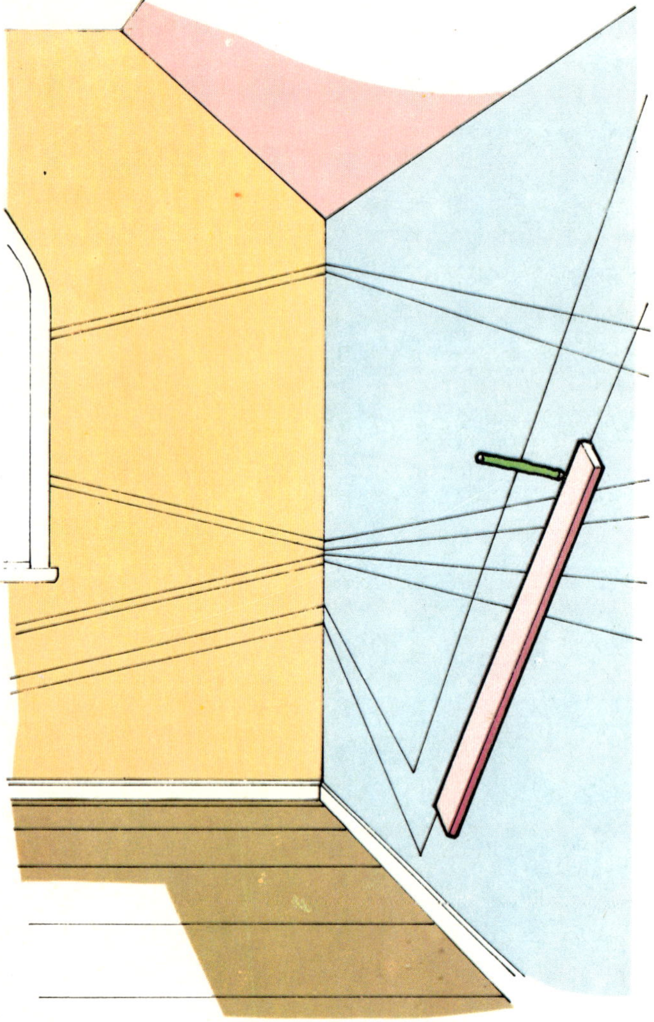

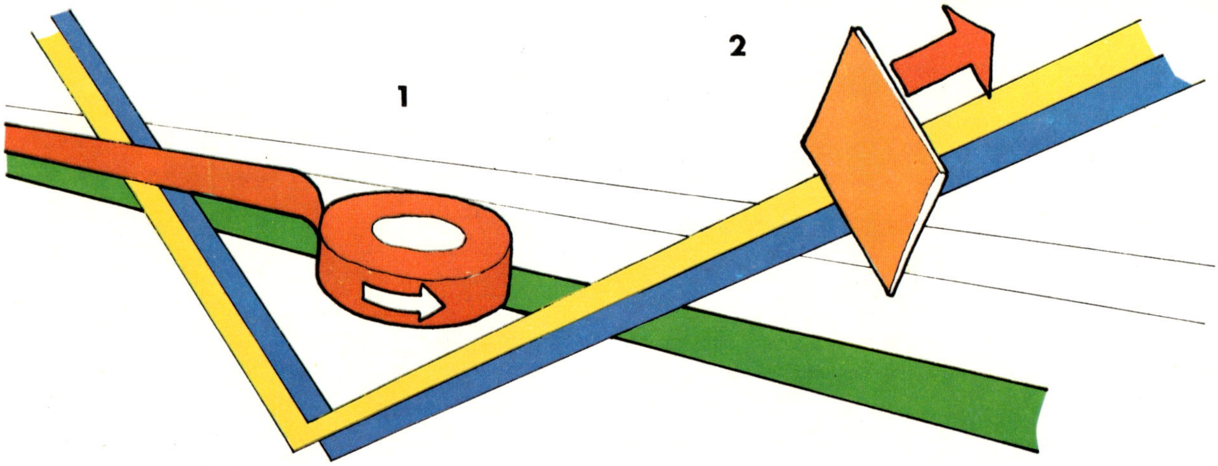

You will first have to decide upon the colours of tape and the design that will suit your own room. Next, work out the design for each wall on paper.
Long horizontal lines will make the room appear longer and lower; vertical and upward sloping lines will add height to the room.
It is important to get the lines running straight and the tape stuck smoothly with no uneven places.

1 With the pencil and ruler, mark guide lines for your design on the wall.

2 Stick the chosen coloured tapes along the guide lines.

3 Press the tape down firmly with the edge of the piece of stiff card.

POP CUSHIONS

You will need:

coloured cloth
paper and pencil
scissors pins
needle and thread
scissors

Egg cushion
Enlarge the various pieces you need (a, b and c) onto paper to make patterns. Pin the patterns to the cloth. Cut out 2 pink shapes in white cloth and one each of the yellow shapes in yellow cloth. Sew the white pieces together to make a cushion case, leaving a small opening for the stuffing. Turn this case inside out. Stuff it.

Sew the 2 yellow pieces together. Turn them inside out and stuff the yellow case.

Sew the yellow cushion 'c' side down to the centre of the white cushion to make your egg.

Tube cushion
Enlarge the various pieces a–g onto paper to make patterns. Pin the patterns to the cloth. Cut out 2 green pieces and one each of all the other pieces.

Sew the 2 short sides of the 'f' and 'g' pieces so that they make two tubes. Join these two tubes to form the main body of the cushion. Turn the end of 'g' over, cut a strip of card and sew it into the turning.

Stuff the main body of the cushion. Sew the circular 'c' bit onto the top of 'f'.

Roll and sew 'b' into a small cylinder.

Sew the 2 'a' pieces together leaving an opening to which you join the 'b' cylinder.

Stuff this 'a–b' section of the cushion.

Sew the 'a–b' section onto 'c' so that it forms the opening and overflowing contents of the tube.

Sew the 'd' and 'e' pieces to the tube as decoration. You may of course decide to use different colours and different decorations for your cushion. You could, for instance, match it to an actual brand tube.

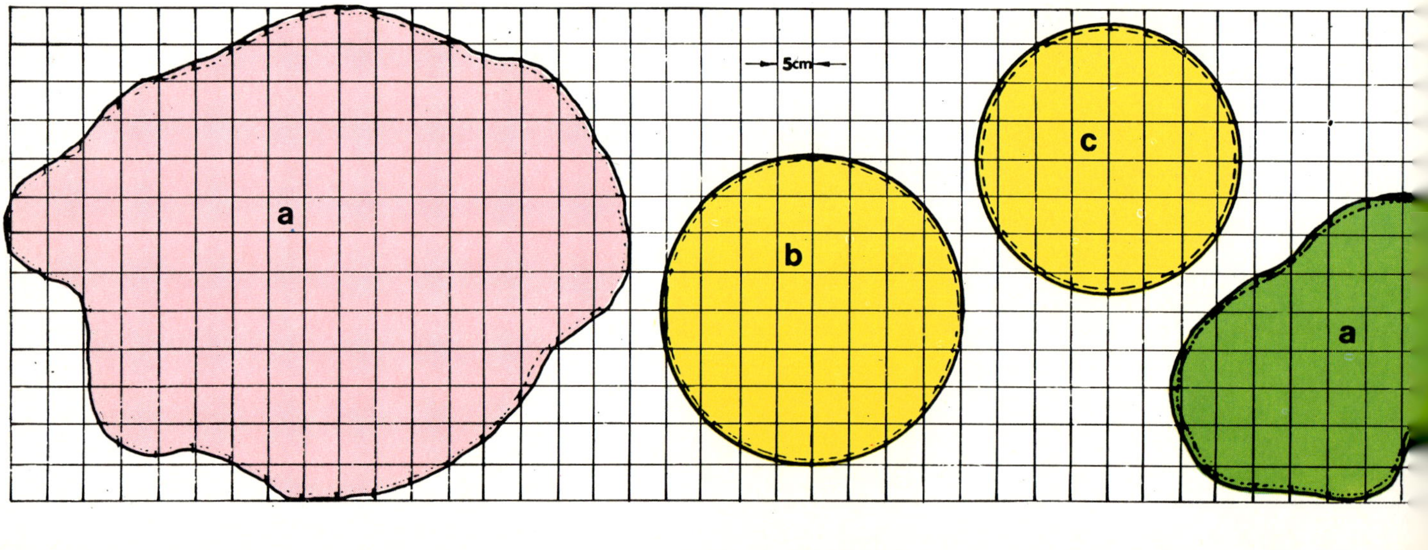

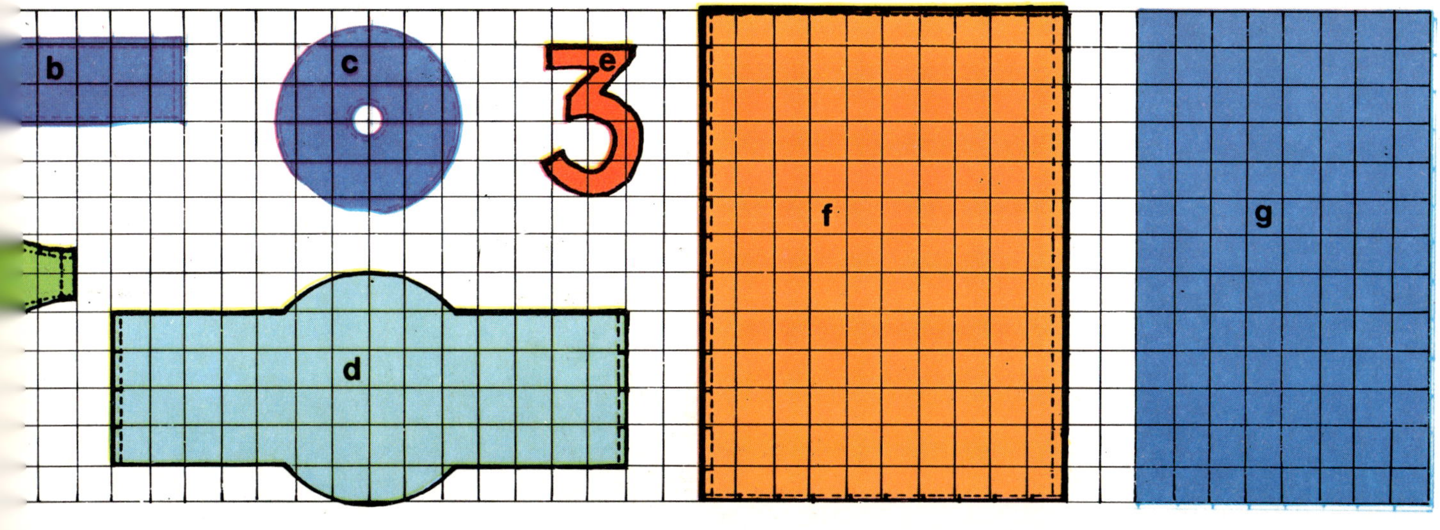
b
c
e
f
g
d

TIGER RUG

You will need:

orange and brown felt
paper pencil scissors
stuffing material
needle and thread
wool

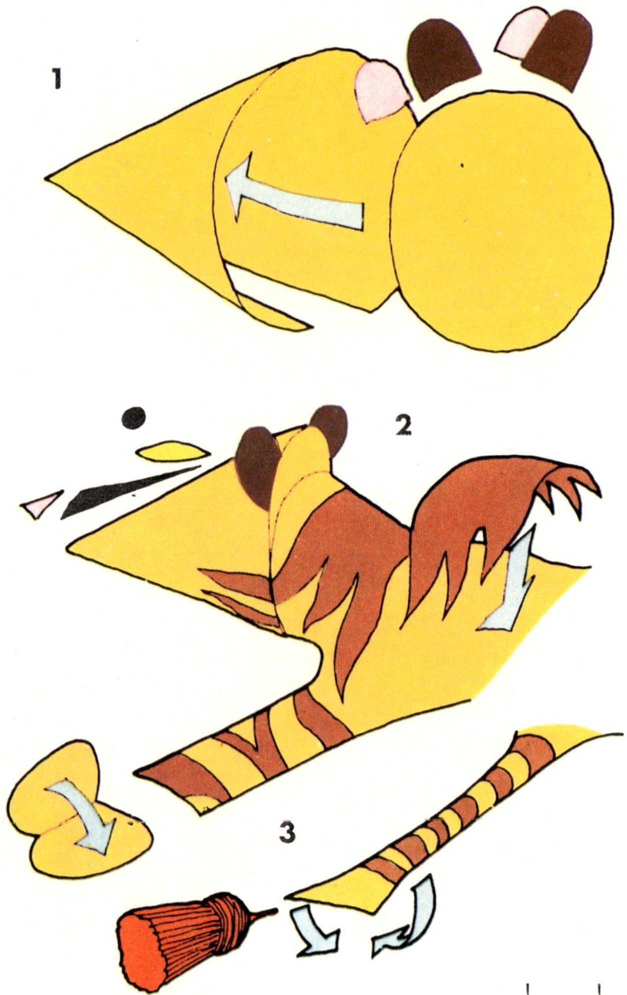

Enlarge the shapes of the tiger on to paper to make a pattern. Cut out the basic shapes of the tiger from the orange felt.

1 Sew the cone-shaped head together along the side. Stuff it. Cut out pieces of felt for the eyes and nose and sew them on to the face. Cut out pieces of felt for the ears and sew them on to the head between the circle of felt and the head cone.

2 Cut out 4 egg-shaped pieces of brown felt for the paws. Sew them folded in half and stuff them. Sew the paws on to the legs.
Cut out stripes from the brown felt and sew them on to the body, legs and tail.
Sew the body to the head with some stripes overlapping on to the neck and head.

3 Make a tassel of lengths of wool and sew it on to the end of the tail.

3
COLT

CANDLE MAKING

INSTRUCTIONS

You will need 90% paraffin wax to 10% stearin, wax dye discs, wick, rod, 2 saucepans, thermometer, basin. You can use different containers for candle moulds: plastic ice trays, cardboard boxes, tins, tin foil etc.

1 Tie the wick loosely round a rod. Balance the rod on the rim of the mould.

2 Heat the wax to 180°F, 65°C.

3 Melt the dye and stearin together. Add them to the wax when it has reached 180°F, 65°C.

4 Pour the wax into the mould leaving a bit in the pan. Allow air bubbles to rise to the surface. Place mould in the basin of cold water.

5 A well will form in the wax as it cools. Let the wax set. Top up with the left-over wax heating it again to 180°F, 65°C.

6 Allow the wax to set before removing your candle from the mould.

Warning: Wax catches fire easily and burns like hot fat. Do not turn the heat up too high or overfill the pan.

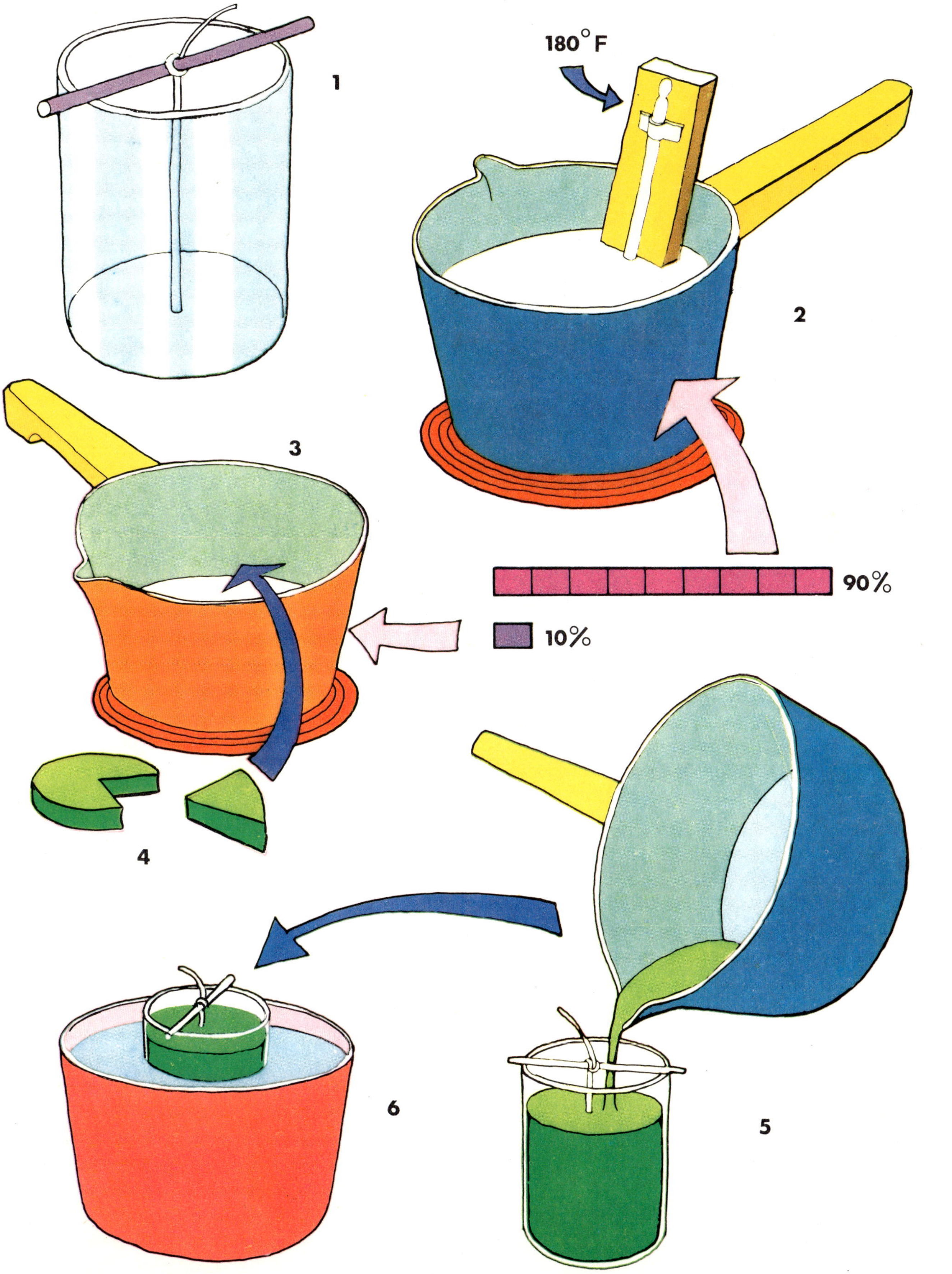
1
180°F
2
3
90%
10%
4
6
5

WATER CANDLES

You will need:

candle wax   wick
ice cube tray
2 rods
bowl
water

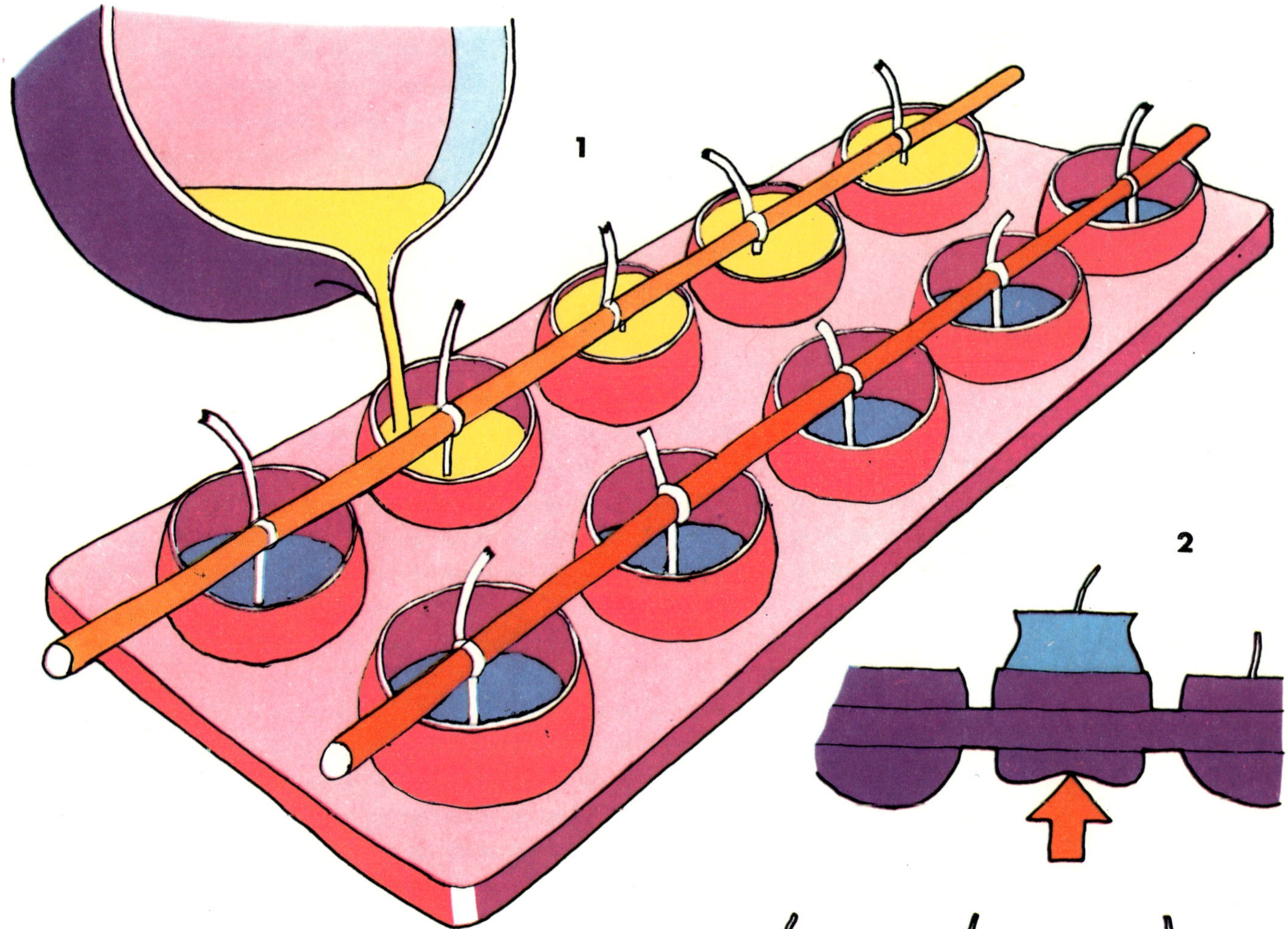

1 Fix the wicks in position on the ice-tray. Fill each division with two different colours of wax.

2 When the wax is set, pop the candles up out of the divisions.

Float the candles in a bowl of water. They will float higher as they melt.

CANDLE FLOWERS

You will need:

pastry cases
candle wax   wick
small rods or straws
wire
metal spoon

1 Fix the wicks in place in the pastry cases. Then fill the cases with candle wax.

2 When the wax has set, add touches of contrasting or darker coloured wax as decoration. You can melt these small quantities of wax in a metal spoon.

3 Take some lengths of wire. Heat the ends and gently melt into the base of the flowers to make the stalks. Allow the stalks to set firmly.
Plant your candle flowers in a flower pot of damp sand so that they will stand upright and the candle wax will drop onto the sand.

1

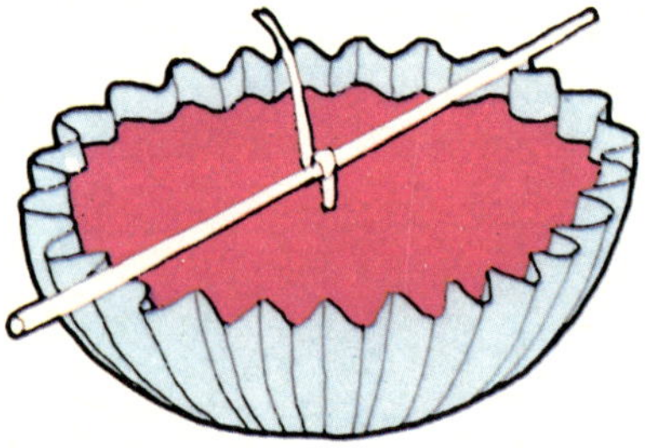

2

3

CANDLE TRAIN

You will need:

candle wax wick
ice cube tray
rod
cutting tool
card tape pins
matchbox
drawing pins

1 Cut lengths of wick long enough to tie loosely round the rod and drop to the base of each division of the tray.
Pour wax into each division. Fill the first division about 80% full and the others with less.

2 Top up each division with different coloured wax.

3 Now make 2 cylindrical moulds from card and tape: one to make the boiler of the engine, the other for the chimney and wheel hubs.

4 Fill these moulds and the base of the matchbox with wax.

5 When the moulds have set, join the boiler to the base with pins.
Cut the other mould into slices.
Pin the chimney on the boiler.
Cut circles of card for the wheels.
Fix the wheel hubs and wheels onto the engine with drawing pins.

Stand the carriages in line behind the engine. Your candle train can be made up of the engine and only one or two carriages or it can be long enough to stretch right along a shelf or down the centre of a table.

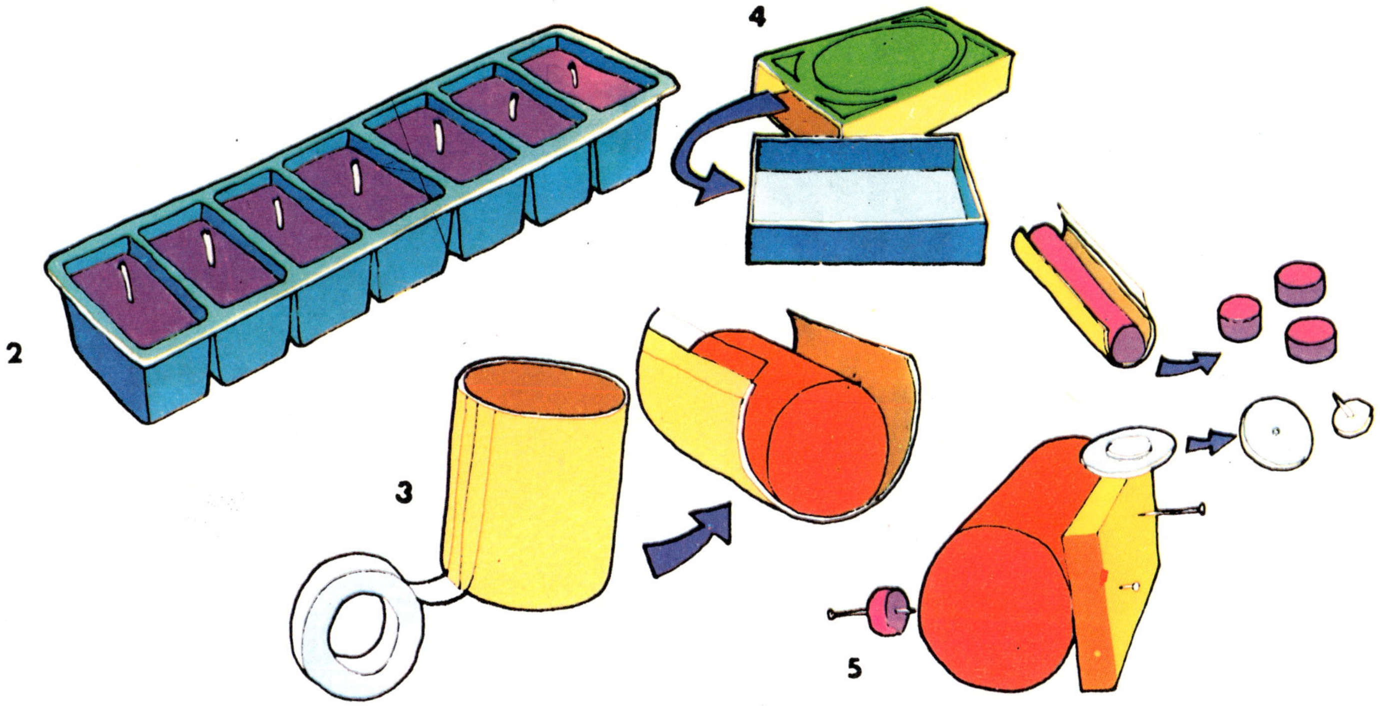
4
2
3
5

CANDLE HOUSE

You will need:

candle wax   wick
card   sticky tape
cutting tool   rod
metal tray
paint and paint brush

1 Prepare the sides of a mould in the shape of a house from pieces of card cut to the shapes and dimensions shown in the diagram.

2 Tape the pieces of the house together firmly. Tie one end of the wick through the roof to hold it in position.

3 Turn the mould upside down. Suspend the bottom of the wick through the house from the rod. Fill the house mould with wax.

4 Use the metal tray (or plate) as a mould for the base. Fill it with green coloured wax to represent grass.

5 When the wax is set firmly, decorate the house with paint. You could use self-adhesive stickers for additional decoration.

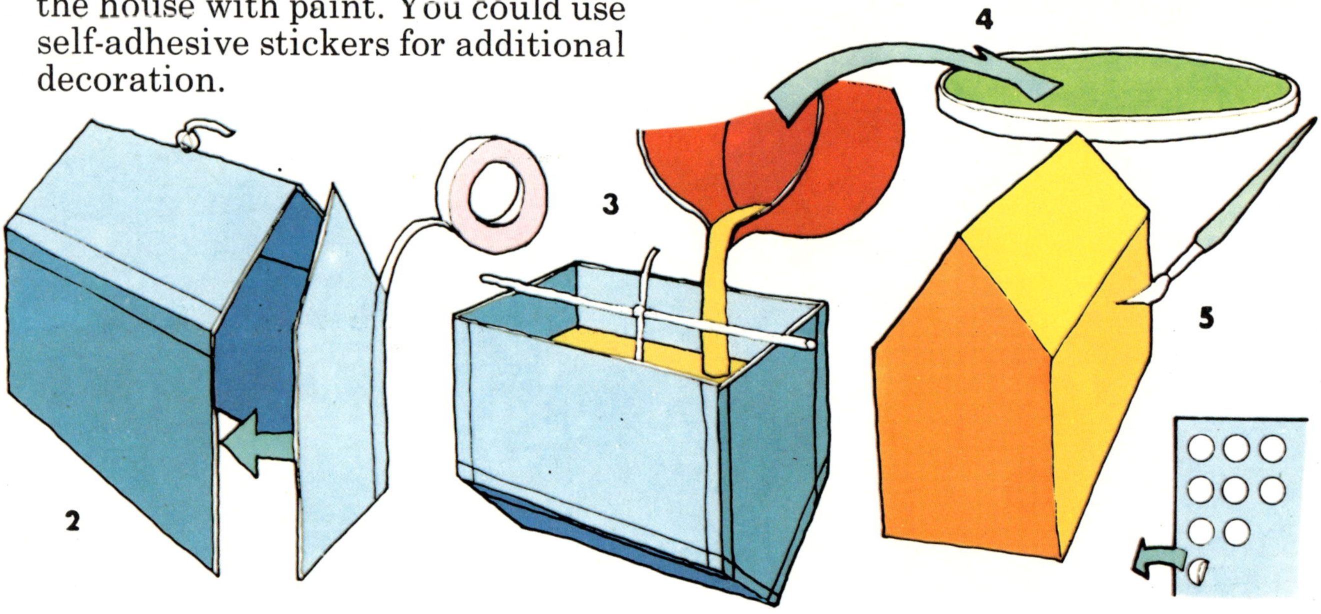

CANDLE CAKE

You will need:

jelly moulds
nail hammer
candle wax
wick
spoon
rod
ice tray

1 You will need two jelly moulds, one larger than the other. Fill the larger mould with candle wax.

2 Punch a hole through the smaller mould for the wick. (You could use a tin foil bowl instead of spoiling a jelly mould.)

3 Suspend the wick in the smaller mould and fill it with wax.

4 When the two main moulds are set, melt some white or creamy coloured wax in a spoon.

5 Join the two main parts of the cake with the white wax so that it looks like a cream filling.

6 Make a red wax cherry in the ice tray as described for the floating candles. Fix it on the top of your cake.

1

2

3

4

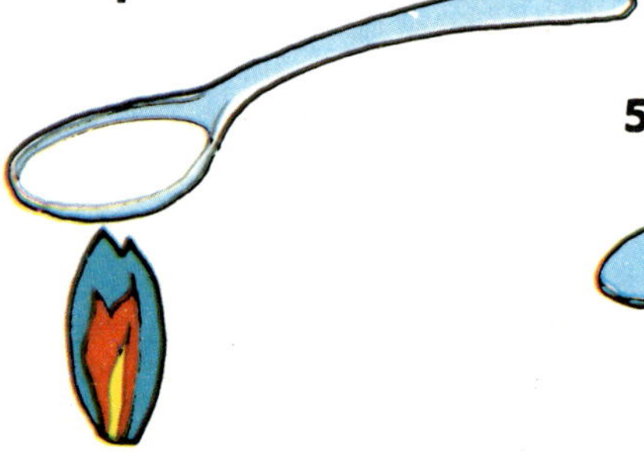

5

6

INDEX